CHIVALRY IN ENGLISH LITERATURE
CHAUCER, MALORY, SPENSER
AND SHAKESPEARE

CHIVALRY
IN ENGLISH LITERATURE
CHAUCER, MALORY, SPENSER
AND SHAKESPEARE

BY

WILLIAM HENRY SCHOFIELD

72517

AMS PRESS
NEW YORK

The Library of Congress cataloged this title as follows:

Schofield, William Henry, 1870-1920.
    Chivalry in English literature: Chaucer, Malory, Spenser, and
Shakespeare. New York, AMS Press ₍1970₎

    x, 294 p. 23 cm.

    Reprint of the 1912 ed.
    Includes bibliographical references.

    1. Chivalry in literature. 2. English literature—Early modern, 1500-1700—
History and criticism.   I. Title.

PR149.C5S4   1970   820.9′353   72-137289
ISBN 0-404-05621-0   MARC

Library of Congress   71₍74₎

Reprinted from the edition of 1912, Cambridge
First AMS edition published in 1970

Manufactured in the United States of America

AMS PRESS, INC.
NEW YORK, N.Y.

TO THE MEMORY OF MY MASTER

GASTON PARIS

MEMBER OF THE FRENCH ACADEMY

SCHOLAR AND GENTLEMAN

PREFACE

THE following lectures were delivered in French at the Sorbonne, and in English at the University of Copenhagen, during the spring of 1911. They have been revised and enlarged for publication. Part of the last lecture appeared in the *Revue de Paris* (July 1, 1911) under the heading *Le "Gentleman" dans Shakespeare.*

I take this opportunity to express publicly my high appreciation of the honour done me by the great institutions of learning above mentioned in their invitations to address them, and also of the generous courtesy with which I was received by their officers and students.

The proofs of the volume have been read by my colleagues, Professors Wendell, Kittredge, and Neilson. I am much indebted to them for this service, and for their friendly criticism.

W. H. S.

East Hill
Peterborough, N. H.
October, 1912

CONTENTS

CONTENTS

love : Platonism and Puritanism : Characters in the " Faery Queen" —
Braggadochio, Sir Calidore: New combination of learning and chivalry:
The scholar and the gentleman : Sidney a true model of "worth" :
" Abeunt studia in mores."

SHAKESPEARE
Shakespeare and Spenser: Shakespeare's character and view of himself:
Mediaeval sentiment in " The Rape of Lucrece" : Outer aspects of chiv-
alry in various works : Lord Herbert of Cherbury and Hector : Fair
play : The poet's emphasis on "honour" : Brutus: Knightly figures in
historical plays : Hotspur and Prince Hal : Falstaff : The "Order of
Chivalry" and the "Law of Arms" : Degenerate knights : Hamlet and
Laertes : Court versus country : "As You Like It" : Shakespeare's joy in
gentleness : Chivalric love prefigured that which he exalted : His pre-
sentation of love similar to Chaucer's, unlike Bacon's : Some of his
heroines : "Romeo and Juliet" : His thoughts on the relations of blood
and virtue, fortune and merit, art and nature, honour and goodness :
The characteristics of gentlemen : A summary comparison of the atti-
tudes of Chaucer, Malory, Spenser, and Shakespeare towards chivalry.

CONCLUSION
Contrast of French and English chivalry : The English ideal of the
gentleman : "English history is aristocracy with the doors open" :
Washington and America : Chivalry and Christianity : Chivalry to-day.

NOTES

INTRODUCTION

INTRODUCTION

CHIVALRY is less an institution than an ideal. This fact is set forth clearly by Léon Gautier in his distinguished book, *La Chevalerie*. An eminent English critic, John Addington Symonds, has written to the same effect:*

"Chivalry is not to be confounded with feudalism. Feudalism was a form of social organization based upon military principles. Chivalry was an ideal binding men together by participation in potent spiritual enthusiasms. Feudalism was the bare reality of mediaeval life. Chivalry was the golden dream of possibilities which hovered above the eyes of mediaeval men and women, ennobling their aspirations, but finding its truest expression less in actual existence than in legend and literature. The pages of feudal history tell a dismal tale of warfare, cruelty, oppression, and ill-regulated passions. The chivalrous romances present sunny pictures of courtesy and generosity and self-subordination to exalted aims. It is always thus. The spirit wars against the flesh, the idea against the fact, in the lives of nations as well as of individuals. Christianity itself, in theory, is far different from the practice of the Christian commonwealths. Yet, who shall say that the spirit in this

* Wherever an asterisk occurs in the text, a note will be found at the end of the book.

warfare is not real, or that the idea is impotent? that Christianity, though never practised in its whole integrity, is not the very salt and essence of the life of modern nations? Even so chivalry, though rarely realized in its pure beauty, though scarcely to be seized outside the songs of poets, and the fictions of romancers, was the spiritual force which gave its value to the institutions and the deeds of feudalism. Whatever was most noble in the self-devotion of Crusaders; most beneficial to the world in the foundation of the knightly orders; most brilliant in the lives of Richard, the Edwards, Tancred, Godfrey of Bouillon; most enthusiastic in the lives of Rudel, Dante, Petrarch; most humane in the courtesy of the Black Prince; most splendid in the courage of Bayard; in the gallantry of Gaston de Foix; in the constancy of Sir Walter Manny; in the loyalty of Blondel; in the piety of St. Louis—may be claimed by the evanescent and impalpable yet potent spirit which we call chivalry.

"Regarding chivalry, not as an actual fact of history, but as a spiritual force, tending to take form and substance in the world at a particular period, we find that its very essence was enthusiasm of an unselfish kind. The true knight gave up all thought of himself. At the moment of investiture he swore to renounce the pursuit of material gain; to do nobly for the mere love of nobleness; to be generous of his

goods; to be courteous to the vanquished; to redress
wrongs; to draw his sword in no quarrel but a just
one; to keep his word; to respect oaths; and, above
all things, to protect the helpless and to serve women.
The investiture of a knight was no less truly a con-
secration to high unselfish aims for life than was the
ordination of a priest."

The precepts of mediaeval chivalry were never
kept distinct from those of mediaeval Christianity;
on the contrary, the former were carefully fashioned
to make the latter prevail. As a result, early writers
on chivalry strongly insisted that a knight should
possess certain virtues, such as mercy, meekness, and
pity, in addition to loyalty, faithfulness, and truth,
which are an essential part of any Christian code.
They called upon the "brave conquerors" of past
days to wage as fierce an inward war on the Seven
Deadly Sins and "the huge army of the world's desires," as to oppose with all their might the enemies
of the Faith. "The history of chivalry," said Baron
Kervyn de Lettenhove, "is naught else but the picture of the admirable influence exercised by literature, in the name of religion and civilization, on the
violent and brutal passions encouraged and propa-
gated by war. If Froissart and the other chroniclers
or poets of his time admire and exalt chivalry so
highly, it is because they perceive that in subjecting
kings themselves to the duties of chivalry, and in

placing the whole career of a knight between the
two extreme limits of the romance which was read
to him in his youth, and the chronicle by which his
life was judged at its end, they succeeded in giving
to letters in the feudal world a more exalted place
than that which they had ever attained in Greece or
Rome."* Chivalry owed its first sway to the wisdom
of those mediaeval writers who grasped the opportunity it provided to soften the hearts of rough
warriors and restrain any addiction on their part to
cruelty, revenge, and boast. Happily, they had power
to make the watchword "In the Name of Honour"
seem coincident with "In His Name," and were
able to perform miracles of regeneration by grafting
Christ-like tenderness on man-like force. In England,
later, chivalry, like Orpheus' lute, was "strung with
poets' sinews." There, from the fourteenth century
to our own, it has been effectively advanced by men
of letters with moral design.

My object in these lectures is to show, if I can,
by an examination of the life and works of four
celebrated English writers, how the ideal of French
chivalry entered into English literature and thereby
affected the attitude of the English-speaking world.
I shall endeavour to explain why this ideal under-
went certain modifications in its adopted home, so
that it led to a somewhat different conception of
aristocratic conduct from that to which it owed its

origin, and how, thus modified, it still determines our standards for a "gentleman."

The four writers to whom I have referred are Chaucer, Malory, Spenser, and Shakespeare—the chief writers of their times who have had a permanent influence on the sentiments of the English race. They are as unlike as could well be in style and temperament; but they have this in common, to the advantage of our grouping, that they all loved chivalry sincerely, with glad recognition of its noble aim.

Chaucer's attitude towards chivalry one may define as pragmatic, Malory's as romantic, Spenser's as esoteric, and Shakespeare's as historic. If these distinctions are just, they imply a large variety in the presentation of the theme, a striking diversity in emphasis on its salient features, a splendid manifestation of its power of appeal.

CHAUCER

CHAUCER

CHAUCER, while he lived, won the hearts of his fellow men. Faithful disciples called him "master," with evident joy. "My master Chaucer," wrote Lydgate, "was the ground of well-saying. No one old or young in his day was worthy to hold his inkhorn. Yet never in all his life did he hinder another's 'making.' Though he found full many a spot, he would never grumble, or pinch his praise, but always said the best, suffering goodly of his gentleness full many a thing embraced with rudeness." "O master dear and father reverend!" exclaimed Occleve, with like sincere emotion; "from thee I was wont to have counsel and rede. Thou wouldst fain have taught me, but I was young and learned right naught." "With heart as trembling as the aspen leaf," he openly bewailed the poet's death. "Queen of Heaven!" he prayed, "be thou his advocate." "As thou well knowest, O blessed Virgin! with loving heart and high devotion, in thine honour, he wrote full many a line. Make known now unto thy Son how he thy servant was, Maiden Mary, and let his love flower and fructify." Chaucer's personal qualities drew men unto him. His gentleness, based upon his loving heart and high devotion, made him honoured and beloved. Like his own Clerk, gladly would he teach. He loyally served the "Queen of Comfort," and himself gave comfort to mankind.

Here we shall not consider the poet's careful art or wide scope, his subtlety in psychological analysis or power of vivid description, his unsurpassed skill as a painter of human beings, or even his captivating humour. We shall enquire only how he came to be enamoured of "gentilesse," how his poems reveal the practices and precepts of the knightly class in his age, and how his character, as early developed by his environment and reading, and later by broad experience of the world, finally affected his views of nobility. Chaucer, we shall see, was not only "the first finder of our fair language;" he was the first finder of our chivalry.*

I

IN 1338, at most two years before the poet's birth, his father, John Chaucer, a well-to-do citizen of London, was in attendance on King Edward III and Queen Philippa during their memorable expedition to Flanders and Cologne; and ten years later he was still, or again, in the royal service, deputy to the king's butler at the port of Southampton. John Chaucer, it seems, was born in the same year as Edward III (1312), and must early have felt the appeal of that eager chivalric life which the king pursued. He could hardly have failed to fix his son's

attention on the doings of the Black Prince, Sir
John Chandos, Sir Walter Manny, and various other
knights, who, as Froissart states, were "reputed sov-
ereigns in all chivalry," and urge him

> *to comune with [every] gentil wight*
> *Ther he mighte lerne gentilesse aright.*

It was probably he who brought it about that Geoffrey started his career at court.*

Unfortunately, Chaucer has left us no account of
his boyhood, as Froissart did, and we have no posi-
tive information concerning him before 1357. Important records, however, show that he was then
a page in the household of the handsome Lionel,
Duke of Clarence, and his charming wife, Elizabeth
of Ulster, ward of the queen, who had been married as children, and were now hardly older than the
poet himself. "It would appear," said Dr. Bond, who
first called attention to these records, that Chaucer
"was at that period at Hatfield in Yorkshire; that
he was present at the celebration of the feast of
St. George, at Edward III's court, in attendance on
the Countess, in April of that year; that he followed
the court to Woodstock; and that he was again at
Hatfield, probably from September, 1357, to the end
of March, 1358, and would have witnessed there
the reception of John of Gaunt, then Earl of Rich-
mond. We may infer that he was present at that

most splendid entertainment given by Edward III to the royal personages then in England,—including the King of France, the Queen of Scotland, the King of Cyprus, and that saddest of figures in such a scene, the sister of the captive King of France and Edward's own mother, the almost-forgotten Queen Isabella,—at what was ever after called the Great Feast of St. George, in the same year; and that he was at Reading with the court and at London in the following winter."

The time was one of intense excitement. The battle of Poictiers, which had just been fought, had sent a thrill of exultation and pride throughout the nation. Everyone was speaking of the Black Prince, who, although he had fought all the morning against his enemy "like a fell and cruel lion," yet treated him when the battle was over with almost fabulous courtesy, waiting upon him at table, and declaring that the King of France had borne himself more bravely than anyone on the field. All were now awaiting the return of the Prince, with his royal prisoner, in an ecstasy of excitement. Finally, after an eleven days' voyage from Bordeaux, he landed at Sandwich, and rode straight to Canterbury, where he offered thanks at the shrine of St. Thomas, and then went on to London by the same route as Chaucer's pilgrims. This triumphal procession, marked by most picturesque incidents, must have made an ineffaceable impression on the young man. And soon he was himself to participate in actual war.

The Dauphin having rejected the agreement made by his father, King John was imprisoned, and all Englishmen between the ages of sixteen and sixty were commanded to make ready to join Edward in war against France. Immense stores of provisions were quickly collected, and in October, 1359, a brilliant army set forth, crossed the Channel, and proceeded to Rheims and Paris.

Like his Squire, Chaucer now journeyed in arms through Artois and Picardy. Unluckily, he was taken prisoner in a skirmish near Rethel, but was ransomed soon after by the king, who paid a considerable sum to this end. He was probably with the army on the eighth of May, at the signature of the Treaty of Brétigny, by which Edward renounced his claim to the throne of France. He was in Calais when King John, now set free, came there to meet Edward, and he participated in the fortnight of fêtes that followed. From his deposition in a law-suit later, we are certain that at this time he was observant of heraldry.

> *Tower'd cities please* [*him*] *then,*
> *And the busy hum of men,*
> *When throngs of knights and barons bold*
> *In weeds of peace high triumphs hold,*
> *With store of ladies, whose bright eyes*
> *Rain influence, and judge the prize*

Of wit, or arms, while both contend
To win her grace, whom all commend.

Thus:

Pomp and feast and revelry,
With mask and antique pageantry,

which appeared to Milton

Such sights as youthful poets dream
On summer eves by haunted stream,

were actualities of the young Chaucer's life.*

We next hear of him in 1367, when he is granted a good pension, as a "beloved yeoman" in the king's household. Before this he had been married to one of the ladies-in-waiting of Queen Philippa, named Philippa after her, who at the same time is also granted a pension for life. Through his wife Chaucer undoubtedly increased his influence at court, for she was a sister of Katherine Swynford, who eventually became John of Gaunt's wife. On various later occasions Philippa Chaucer received royal grants, because of her "good and agreeable service" to Edward's queen. On August 15, 1369, that virtuous lady died, whereupon, to both Chaucer ("a squire of less estate") and his wife, special allowance was made for weeds of mourning. On September 12 the queen's favourite daughter-in-law, Blanche, Duchess of Lancaster, also died, at the age of twenty-nine, and in memory of her the poet soon after composed his first notable work, the *Book of the Duchess*. The death of Queen Philippa and the Duchess Blanche closed a very significant period in the life of Chaucer. He was then nearly, if not quite, thirty years old. By this time the chief features of his personality were undoubtedly fixed.

We are happy to have Froissart's help in determining the atmosphere of Philippa's court. The young Flemish writer had journeyed there in 1361, bearing with him a rhymed chronicle of the wars of the period, of which he says: "I presented the volume to my lady Philippa of Hainault, noble Queen of England, who right amiably received it, to my great profit and advancement." "God has given me so much grace," he elsewhere states, "that I have been of the household of King Edward and the noble queen his wife, my lady Philippa of Hainault, whose clerk I was in my youth and whom I served with fair ditties and amorous treatises." "For the love of the noble and valiant lady whom I served, all great lords, kings, dukes, counts, barons and knights, to whatever nation they belonged, loved me and saw me willingly."

"Tall and upright was she," writes Froissart, "wise, gay, humble, pious, liberal and courteous, decked and adorned in her time with all noble virtues, beloved of God and of mankind." In the *Fair Boscage of Youth*,* where he singles out several of his former friends for praise, he begins with her; for, as he states, she "created and made" him. Next to Philippa in the same poem, Froissart places Blanche of Lancaster, whom he describes as:

> *Gaie, lie, friche, esbatans,*
> *Douce, simple, d'umble semblance.*

"Tant suis plein de mélancholie," says the poet, "j'ai trop perdu en ces deux dames."

Chaucer never once mentions Queen Philippa by name, any more than he does Edward III, the Black Prince, or almost any great personage of the realm; but it is most probable that he felt towards her, as towards Blanche, much as Froissart did. In any case, the *Book of the Duchess* gives us a definite impression of what he then thought noble in woman.

Chaucer's portrait of Blanche is the first life-like picture in English literature of an actual English lady. In her he portrayed gladness, friendliness, sweetness, *debonaireté*, but no quality at odds with straightforward honesty and loyal wifely devotion. The fact is emphasized that though Blanche had radiant physical charm, and dullness dreaded her, yet she was not coquettish, let alone frivolous. She would never put herself in an equivocal position, nor encourage men's attentions, nor hold out false hopes. She used no such small tricks. She was never in the least scornful to anyone. She was the resting-place of truth. Good folk over all others she loved. She used gladly to do well.

I saw hir daunce so comlily,
Carole and singe so swetely,
Laughe and pleye so womanly,
And loke so debonairly,
So goodly speke and so frendly,
That certes, I trow, that evermore
Nas seyn so blisful a tresore.

Blanche was trained by Philippa, and it is believed that the two were exceptionally sympathetic.
They died within a month of each other, and were
inevitably associated in the poet's memory. When,
then, he was called upon by John of Gaunt, a living
patron, to commemorate the loss of Blanche, and
undertook, in the *Book of the Duchess,* to describe
an ideal gentlewoman, he could hardly have failed to
think not only of her, but also of her beloved guide.
The epitaph on Philippa's tomb, after a description
of her virtues, closes with the words: "Learn to live."
It appears as if it were particularly from Philippa,
whom all in her time proclaimed "the Good," that
the pure in heart at the English court learned to live.
Probably from her Chaucer first gained that profound
respect for good women which is manifest in all his
works.*

For several years subsequent to Philippa's death,
Chaucer and his wife remained closely attached to
the court, both probably in the employ of John of
Gaunt and his new duchess. In 1374, on St. George's
Day at Windsor, when as usual the Knights of the

Garter were holding high festival, the king made to Chaucer ("dilecto armigero nostro") a new grant of a pitcher of wine daily. One is glad to know that the poet retained Edward's regard to the end. But there can be little doubt what he thought of Alice Perrers, who had taken Philippa's place. In the same year, 1374, at a great seven days' tournament held at Smithfield, the king's vain mistress appeared at his side, dressed in gorgeous raiment as the Lady of the Sun! Immediately after the Windsor festival, Chaucer took a life-lease of a house above Aldgate in London. On June 8 he was given a lucrative position in the custom house, and then apparently settled down to routine occupation in the city. But he was not confined altogether by business duties. Between 1370 and 1380 he was employed on no less than seven diplomatic missions to various lands—France, Flanders, and Italy—by which without question his knowledge grew, his acquaintance with literature broadened, and his mind matured. In 1377 Edward III died a melancholy death, just a year after his illustrious son, the Black Prince; and Richard II, a youth of eleven years, reigned in his stead. Then for some time John of Gaunt and his two brothers were guardians of the throne. Men began to lament: "Woe to thee, O land, where thy king is a child."

II

IF we review Chaucer's productions up to this point in his life, we shall find that they exhibit him as a man of pure, idealistic character.

"His earliest extant complete poem," the so-called *A. B. C.*, which is said to have been written for the Duchess Blanche, reveals whole-hearted devotion to the "almighty and most merciful queen," gentle yet glorious, mother of Our Lord. It is significant that this prayer is all that the poet extracted from the Monk Deguilleville's ponderous allegory *The Pilgrimage of Human Life*, and that he heightened the effect of his original by new thoughts finely phrased. It is also significant that one of the chief passages in Dante which appealed to him was the Invocation to Mary at the close of the *Paradiso*. Chaucer was drawn to it not only because of its great beauty of expression, but also because of his sympathy for the feeling there enshrined. Both he and Dante adored the Virgin because in her mercy, goodness, and pity were "assembled with magnificence." She had borne the Son of Man within the "blissful cloister" of her sides. Chaucer understood well the mystical devotion of St. Bernard, to whose hymns in Mary's honour he refers with applause. He makes his heroine Constance tenderly appeal to her for help in lonely grief:

Now, lady bright, to whom alle woful cryën,
Thou glorie of wommanhede, thou faire may,
Thou haven of refut, brighte sterre of day,
Rewe on my child, that of thy gentilesse
Rewest on every rewful in distresse!

The Virgin's "gentilesse" was gloried in by all gentle folk on earth. They envisaged her as the Venus of Heaven; they exalted her as the divine patroness of chivalry. Chaucer seems to have viewed the Virgin as a living ideal of womanhood. In her was abounding pity; she had a tender heart; she was the great treasurer of bounty to mankind—"glorious maid and mother, which wert never bitter, but full of sweetness and of mercy ever."

Chaucer's life of St. Cecilia is a close translation, and one cannot infer much from it as to the poet's own sentiments. He reveals, however, no cynicism or impatience in his version of this ecclesiastical fable, and was apparently glad to show how by baptism men might become "Christ's own knights," cast away all the works of darkness, and take on the "armour of brightness." The converts of the tale fought a good fight; they kept the faith; there was laid up for them a crown in Heaven.

Likewise, in the story of Constance, another early work, revised to suit the Man of Law, religion is treated with full respect. Here Christ is glorified as the champion of the weak, the cure of every harm.

The "victorious tree" on which He, "the white Lamb," hung, is the "protection of the true;" through it Constance was saved from manifold distress. The portrait which Chaucer draws of this princess of Rome, wife of King Alla of Northumberland, is that of an ideal character in his own eyes:

> *In hir is heigh beautee, withoute pryde,*
> *Yowthe, withoute grenehede or folye;*
> *To alle hir werkes vertu is hir gyde,*
> *Humblesse hath slayn in hir al tirannye.*
> *She is mirour of alle curteisye;*
> *Hir herte is verray chambre of holinesse,*
> *Hir hand, ministre of fredom for almesse.*

Constance patterned herself on the blissful Mary, holy and benign. The "common voice" declared that it would have been well if she, "to reckon as well her goodness as beauty," had been queen of all Europe.

In the Clerk's Tale, Chaucer again described a young wife of singular nobleness. Griselda was a girl of lowly station, with whom a marquis of Lombardy fell in love. His followers wished him to make a distinguished match; but in his heart he so commended Griselda's womanhood and virtuous beauty, her dignified mien and filial devotion, the absence in her of "likerous lust" —

> *for she wolde vertu plese,*
> *She knew wel labour, but non ydel ese—*

that he determined to marry her on whom his heart

was set. And Griselda, without seeming effort, by simply being benign and "digne of reverence," soon captured everyone's heart—a convincing proof of her true gentleness! "Everyone loved her that looked on her face." But, according to the story, Lord Walter decided to test her fidelity and obedience. So he separated from her first one child, then another, and finally announced that he had arranged to take a new wife, whom he bade her make ready to receive. She accepted all her lord did without complaint, nor showed him any less love than before. She went back in poverty to her cottage home—this "flower of wifely patience"—without revealing any anger, or giving any indication of offence. Whereupon, the poet says:

> No wonder is, for in hir grete estaat
> Hir gost was ever in pleyn humylitee;
> No tendre mouth, non herte delicat,
> No pompe, no semblant of royaltee,
> But ful of pacient benignitee,
> Discreet and prydeles, ay honourable,
> And to hir housbonde ever meke and stable.

Chaucer says that he told the Clerk's Tale to show, not that wives should be humble like Griselda, but that all men and women should be constant in adversity. We should, he declares, accept the will of God, since His chastenings are for our good. Then (as an afterthought, it would seem; for several manuscripts have another ending) the poet relieved the high-wrought nature of the narrative by some ironical comments:

> But o word, lordinges, herkeneth er I go:—
> It were ful hard to finde now a dayes
> In al a toun Grisildes three or two;*
> For, if that they were put to swich assayes,
> The gold of them hath now so badde alayes
> With bras, that thogh the coyne be fair at yë,
> It wolde rather breste a-two than plye.

The poet's constant references to conditions at the time of his writing his several works (not to his own time in general,—the fourteenth century,—as we are too prone to say without reflection) are very significant. His youthful training, as well as his temperament, was idealistic. In his early years he was surrounded by ladies whom he could praise unstintedly for their goodness and patience. But history does not reveal many such in prominent places in the last quarter of the century, when, on the contrary, women abound of the type of Alice Perrers and Kate Mortimer, women more like Lady May and the Wife of Bath. There is in Chaucer a steady comparison of the present with *le bon vieux temps*, which was to him the happy era of Edward III's vigour and Philippa's beauty, when the king won brilliant victories and was faithfully devoted to his queen.

By too exclusive consideration of the gaiety of Chaucer's work, many readers have failed to regard sufficiently the underlying seriousness of his character. Yet this is manifest, not only in his prose works,* but also in poems composed at all stages of his career. Naturally it grew with advancing years, particularly as a result of the steady deterioration of morals among both aristocrats and commoners. Distressing changes in public life forced Chaucer, as well as every other thoughtful man, towards the close of the fourteenth century, to turn away from fair to foul aspects of social and political life. When Froissart returned to England in 1395, after an absence of twenty-eight years, he was disheartened to find the whole atmosphere different from what it had been in the glad days of his youth, and he thus voices the prevailing pessimism: "What have become, they said in England, of such great undertakings and valiant men, splendid battles and conquests? Who are the knights in England who do any such thing? In former days Englishmen were feared and dreaded, and we were spoken of throughout all the world. Now we give cause for silence. It certainly appears that we are in this country weakened in sense and grace. Times have changed from right to wrong since the death of good King Edward. Justice was maintained and guarded with care in his day. At present, King Richard of Bordeaux wishes only repose and rest, frivolities and amusements with ladies. Thus it is apparent that soon there will be no man of valour in England, and all sorts of felony and hate will increase."

"The wise," adds Froissart, "noted the great evils that might be born and come; to them the fools paid no heed." Chaucer was surely among the wise, as all will admit who read his ballade *Lack of Stedfastness*, in which he too laments that "the world [had] made a permutation from right to wrong, from truth to fickleness." Sadly he affirms that a man's word is no longer felt to be an obligation; truth is put down; pity is exiled; no man is merciful; and finally he implores King Richard to cultivate chivalrous attributes:

> *O prince, desyre to be honourable . . .*
> *Dred God, do law, love trouthe and worthinesse,*
> *And wed thy folk again to stedfastnesse.*

One of Chaucer's most impressive poems is a "Ballade de Bon Conseil," entitled *Truth*. "Flee from the press, and dwell with soothfastness;" "tempest thee not all crooked to redress;" "work well thyself, that thou canst others rede;"—these are words of counsel that he spoke with conviction, revealing his own creed.

> *That thee is sent, receyve in buxomnesse,*
> *The wrastling for this worlde axeth a fal.*
> *Her nis non hoom, her nis but wildernesse.*
> *Forth, pilgrim, forth! Forth, beste, out of thy stal!*
> *Know thy contree, look up, thank God of al;*
> *Hold the hye wey, and let thy gost thee lede:*
> *And trouthe shal delivere, hit is no drede.*

In an exalted envoy, the poet pleads with men to
leave their wretchedness, and cry mercy of God, who
in His high goodness made them of naught.

> *Draw unto Him, and pray in general*
> *For thee, and eek for other, hevenlich mede;*
> *And trouthe shal delivere, hit is no drede.*

Truth evidently meant to Chaucer, not merely ve-
racity, but, above that, loyalty, verity, and highest of
all—symbolically—the truth that makes one free.
Truth, indeed, is the very keynote of Chaucer's
poetry—truth in description, which we call realism;
truth in sentiment, namely poise; truth in imagination, that is art; truth to human nature; truth
to truth. "Truth," Chaucer affirmed, "is the highest
thing that man may keep."*

III

THOUGH Chaucer's idealism is marked, it is not
extravagant. Devotion to the Virgin, exaltation of
good women, praise of purity, meekness, stedfastness, and truth were incumbent upon all who strove
to fulfil the high principles of the order of chivalry. Chaucer was high-minded, but he was also
glad-hearted. In later life, as we have seen, he viewed
with anxiety the growing corruption of the times,
but he never rebelled against the existing institutions of society. He sincerely deplored the wrong-
doing of the great, but he never removed from their

sphere. Throughout his career, the poet was thrown into intimate contact with the highest of rank in the realm, and was plainly happy in that environment. His temperament made him a glad witness of pageants, a genial companion of men of the world, a gracious friend of ladies, and a sympathetic listener to all who related adventures or feats of war.

Chaucer was lucky to be born amid the splendours of the reign of Edward III, in the halcyon days of English knighthood. Unquestionably there was much artificiality and affectation in the outer manifestations of chivalry in England, as elsewhere, at that time. Edward III may justly be accused of vainglory in his confident emulation of King Arthur. The elegant Order of the Garter was a far cry from the practical crusading orders of an earlier age. Personal ostentation and pride characterized notable warriors of the period. There was mainly vanity in the new pursuit of heraldry. Yet, notwithstanding this, the era of Chaucer's youth makes a strong appeal to the manly. It was certainly not one of mere make-believe, but of vigorous and effective undertakings. Chivalry then, as men of the day themselves felt, had reached its height, and shone with unsurpassed brilliance. Froissart believed that during the fifty years of which he wrote in his chronicle more "feats of arms and marvels" had taken place in the world than in three hundred years before.

"Since the time of the good King Charlemagne,"
he declared, "never happened so great *aventures de
guerre.*" The spirit of chivalry, without question,
animated heroic oftener than fantastic deeds. In the
general disorder of Christendom, in the era of the
great schism, when prelates and other clergy were
often entitled to scorn, its ideals were the chief guide
of many men in daily conduct. Langland represents
an honest Plowman as the one best fitted to lead his
contemporaries to the shrine of Truth. Chaucer, in
his picture of the same English world, places first
and foremost a noble Knight.

From our present point of view, the portrait of
the Knight in the Prologue to the *Canterbury Tales*
is the most significant single passage in Chaucer.
It has been repeated by historians and critics count-
less times. The vital part of the description of the
Knight is not, however, the statement of far-away
places where he fought. These might have occurred
to anyone as the most suitable for an errant warrior
to visit, and were perhaps suggested by a poem of
Machaut. Few remember them now. It is the character of the noble pilgrim that has permanently held
men's thought. Everyone who knows anything about
Chaucer is familiar with these lines:

> *A Knight ther was, and that a worthy man,*
> *That fro the tyme that he first began*
> *To ryden out, he loved chivalrye, —*

Trouthe and honour, fredom and curteisye.
Ful worthy was he in his lordes werre,
And therto hadde he riden (no man ferre)
As well in Cristendom as hethenesse,
And ever honoured for his worthinesse.

. . . .

And evermore he hadde a sovereyn prys.
And though that he were worthy, he was wys,
And of his port as meke as is a mayde.
He never yet no vileinye ne sayde,
In al his lyf, unto no maner wight.
He was a verray parfit gentil knight.

While considering the features of this portrait, it is well to know that they are not unique. Without in the least assailing the poet's originality, but rather with the idea of emphasizing his genius for improving the already excellent, it may be pointed out that Chaucer's words resemble closely those used by Watriquet de Couvin to describe his patron, Gauchier de Châtillon, Constable of France, who died in 1329.* The standards of chivalry being universal, one or several of the phrases used by Chaucer can be paralleled in many other works; but nowhere else, so far as known, is there a continuous description which can so reasonably be offered as the source of his conception. Watriquet was one of the most notable poets of Hainault, Queen Philippa's home when she became King Edward's wife. He certainly occupied a position of dignity in Gauchier's circle, for he addresses the lords and ladies about him with extraordinary frankness, dwelling upon their duties as gentle folk, while he exalts the honour of their estate. He adored "gentilesse." He was the apostle of "loyalty." There is other evidence that Chaucer knew his work.

In his *Dit du Connestable de France*, Watriquet regularly calls the knight Gauchier a *preud'omme* (worthy man) and highly applauds his *prouesce* (worthiness). He terms him *roi de chevalerie*. We are informed that this worthy man, who loved chivalry, rode out young to foreign lands (Aragon, Sicily, etc.), and sought without repose in many wars *pour aquerre d'honneur le pris.*

> *Sa renomée s'estendi*
> *En mainte marche par le monde.*
>
> *Onques personne tant prisie*
> *De lui a son vivant ne fu.*

Though he was *un preud'omme que chascuns prise*, he was also *sage*.

Near the beginning of the eulogy we read:

> *Li preudons estoit parfais*
> *En honneur par diz et par fais. . . .*
> *Prouesce faisoit esveillier,*
> *Courtoisie, honneur et largesce*
> *Et loiauté, qui de noblesce*
> *Toutes les autres vertus passe.* . . .*
> *Tant fust plains de courouz ne d'ire*
> *Onques n'issi hors de sa bouche*
> *Vilains mos; maniere avoit douche*
> *Plus que dame ne damoisele.*

"Trouthe and honour, fredom and curteisye" is the exact equivalent of *courtoisie, honneur, et largesce et loiauté.* Strangely enough, Chaucer never uses the word "loyalty," though it is common in other fourteenth-century English writers;* for it he always writes "trouthe." "Fredom," of course, signifies *largesse*, generosity. The passage—"never was [he] so full of anger that there issued from his mouth a word of vileinye; his port was meek, more than [that of] a lady or a maid"—is identical in substance with Chaucer's memorable words regarding the Knight's attitude toward others. Elsewhere Watriquet states that Gauchier was *doux comme un pucelle.* This *gentilz connestable, très gentilz prince*, was, he explains, *en parfaite honneur nourris, très parfait* in largess; in his heart sprang the fountain of *parfaite courtoisie.* Gauchier also was a "verray parfit gentil knight." Whether or no Watriquet's portrait influenced Chaucer's, the claim of the latter to reality is strengthened by the fact that it is parallel to one of an actual personage in the author's age.

An additional feature in Chaucer's description which is significant as exhibiting the Knight's character, lies in the statement regarding his equipment: "His horses were good, but he was not gay." No critic has failed to notice how Chaucer makes his effects in description by contrasts. What the Knight was *not* is as striking as what he was. "He was not gay," just as "he never yet no vileinye ne sayde," is emphatic. Chaucer's ideal knight, whose profession might seem to demand splendid array and richly caparisoned horses, eschewed vain apparel and rode only in serviceable armour, which showed signs of hard wear. His "gipoun" was made of mere fustian and his "habergeoun" was "all besmotered." On the other hand, the Monk, who should have had nothing to do with "dainty" horses and fine raiment and rich living, sought particularly these things. He had swift greyhounds, and spared no cost in his preparation for the hunt. "His boots [were] supple, his horses in great estate. . . . His palfrey was as brown as is a berry."

This passage should be brought into connection with words of the Parson in the last of the *Canterbury Tales*. The Parson there dwells upon the outer signs of the deadly sin of pride; not only does pride appear "in speech and countenance," but also "in outrageous array of clothing." "Alas!" he says, "may men not see *in our days*, the sinful costly array of clothing?" "Also the sin of ornament or of apparel is in things that appertain to riding, as in too many delicate horses that be holden for delight, that be so fair, fat, and costly; and also too many a vicious knave that is sustained because of them; in too curious harness, as in saddles, in cruppers, peytrels, and bridles covered with precious clothing and rich, bars and plates of gold and of silver. For which God saith by Zachariah the prophet, 'I will confound the riders of such horses.' These folk take little regard of the riding of God's Son of Heaven, and of His harness when He rode upon an ass, and had no other harness but the poor clothes of His disciples; nor do we read that ever He rode on other beast. I speak this for the sin of superfluity, and not for reasonable honesty, when reason it requireth."

It deserves, in truth, special notice how much Chaucer's portrait of the ideal Knight resembles in fundamental nature his portrait of the ideal Parson. "Rich in holy thought and work," though lowly of estate, the Parson was as faithful a knight of peace as his higher-born companion a knight of war. Many times in adversity he had proved himself worthy of his Master in Heaven. He fulfilled in his own domain every demand of chivalrous precept—"trouthe and honour, fredom and curteisye." He too "waited after no pomp or reverence." By his own demeanour he commended his profession.* Both the Parson and his brother the Plowman, because they followed so closely in the footsteps of Christ, Chaucer pictures as "gentles of honour;" they had "gentilesse of grace."

We fail wholly to realize the significance of Chaucer's exaltation of the Knight, if we do not observe that he was not simply a man of great physical courage and brilliant achievement in war, but the embodiment of very high spiritual excellence. "Blessed are the meek," says the Gospel, and the Knight is nobly meek. He is Christ-like in his behaviour to his fellows. His chivalry is religious through and through. Not in vain had he vowed his first vow when dubbed —faithfully to serve God and Holy Church.

In his description of the Knight Chaucer presents us with an ideal which we may be sure was seldom if ever realized. Very different it would have been if the author of the *Vision of Piers Plowman* had painted the picture. He would probably have exposed the seamy side of the tapestry of knighthood, all the supposed defects upon which certain one-sided English historians of recent times have been pleased to dwell. Instead of portraying the Knight, as he did the Monk, genially but with clear exhibition of his imperfections, Chaucer chose to portray him as without a flaw, and by his own sympathy he has made him so appealing that we feel that all knights are, or should be, like him. Chaucer has fixed forever our conception of knighthood, beautiful, almost holy. Historians without number may tell us: "Knights were not all like that;" and we reply (with some unreason): "No doubt, but here was at least one." It is singular good fortune that the situation is not the reverse, as in the case of the Monk. Without doubt all monks were not like Chaucer's specimen. But there he stood, and afterwards monks in England had to prove the contrary.

The Knight bore arms honourably "in his lord's wars," but these are not dwelt upon; he was less a patriot than a fighter "for our faith." St. Louis would have called him a *preud'omme*, according to his own Christian interpretation of that word. "Master Robert," once said the great Crusader to the founder of the Sorbonne, "I should wish to have the name of *preud'omme* [worthy man], provided I were one . . . for *preud'ommie* [worthiness] is such a great thing and such a good thing that merely to name it fills one's mouth." A *preud'omme*, who believed in God and the Virgin, the King carefully distinguished from ordinary *preus hommes*, who merely showed valour in fight. Of the latter, he pointed out, there were many in Saracen as well as in Christian lands, but to the former God vouchsafed the great benefit and grace that He guarded him from mortal sin in holy service. The *preud'omme's* prowess came to him as a gift of God.* When such an one had gained "sovereyn pris" in war, it was fitting that he should promptly "do his pilgrimage;" on his return home he should at once yield praise and thanksgiving for the mercies of the Lord.

To Chaucer chivalry was a religion, and, in matter of chivalrous sentiment, he is a pronounced moralist. His morality is not obtrusive, as is the case with Watriquet and Gower; but it is there—consciously, efficaciously, and (his countrymen in the

main think) rightly there. Chaucer never scolds*
or sneers, never draws a long face or sets his jaw;
he is the happiest and cheeriest of comrades; but
he never shows that he approves the wrong, and
he persistently shows that he approves the right.
Though frankly a man of the world, a very human
man, who never dreamed of posing as a saint, he
leaves us in no doubt as to his whole-hearted appro-
bation of "good men of religion" within or without
the church.

IV

HAVING thus studied the qualities with which
Chaucer invests the leading "gentle" among his pilgrims, we should now examine the tale given to him
to tell, the poet's chief production "of storial thing
that toucheth gentilesse."

The position of the Knight's Tale at the beginning of the *Canterbury Tales* attests its importance
in the author's eyes; and the extreme felicity of
style which makes it one of the most charming of all
Chaucer's narratives, shows that he wrote it with
as much care as sympathy.

The tale purports to be one of ancient days, concerning Theseus, King of Athens, and his wife Hippolyta, and deals with the fates of two young princes,
Palamon and Arcite, taken in war against Thebes,
and held without ransom. As it happens, both knights

behold almost simultaneously from their prison window the king's sister Emelye in her garden below, and both instantly fall in love with her. Thereupon they languish in hopeless rivalry. After a while, Arcite is released, yet goes home envying Palamon his continued opportunity to see his lady. He manages, however, to return in disguise, and takes humble service with the king; but he is rapidly advanced in rank. One morning, while in the woods bemoaning his plight, he meets Palamon, who has just escaped from prison, and they agree to settle their dispute by a duel on the following day. Theseus, out hunting with his court, discovers them fighting, and, after his first anger is appeased, undertakes to arrange a great tournament a twelvemonth later, to which each suitor may bring one hundred knights to support his cause, promising to the victor the hand of Emelye. The tournament is a magnificent event, and is amply described in preparation and fulfilment. Arcite wins; but, before leaving the lists, is mortally injured by a fall from his horse. The sorrow at this is intense, and the hero is entombed with great sadness and solemnity. Nevertheless, an alliance between Greece and Thebes being desirable, the king later persuades Emelye to marry Palamon, for, as he says, "gentle mercy ought to pass right,"—a maxim of noble chivalry.

Modern critics have dwelt long upon the romance

and minimized the reality of this tale. Properly understood, however, it is one of the best pictures we have of English courtly life in the fourteenth century. Of course, there is something remote to us in the pageantry described; but to most of us all royal display and entertainment is remote. The technical terms inevitably used to make vivid the account of a tournament are strange to the majority; that, however, does not make them less actual at the time when they were on everyone's lips. Mediaeval armour is no longer seen except in museums; mediaeval costumes are familiar to us only through the books of antiquaries; mediaeval manners may seem nowadays stilted or quaint; yet mediaeval armour, costumes, and manners of entertainment were the only ones that Chaucer knew. Furthermore, Chaucer used the language of his day, a day of chivalrous largess, and showed no plebeian desire to "grouch" and say "but,"* no self-conscious solicitude to avoid exaggeration in speech. There is little if any extravagance in the statements of the Knight's Tale that does not find a parallel in contemporary accounts of the happenings of Edward III's reign.

If acquainted with these, one need but glance at the chief personages of the tale to see that under their names men in Chaucer's circle would have recognized portraits no more conventional than poets were then drawing of persons conspicuous to public gaze. The "gentle duke" Theseus, the "lord and governor" of Athens, is described in terms that must have reminded all of Edward III; and few could read of the tender-hearted Hippolyta without thinking of Philippa. The queen interferes but once, and that is to crave pardon for the young warriors whom her husband—evidently prone, like Edward, to sudden wrath—had impulsively condemned to death. The scene is one of great charm, and worthy to be set alongside of that memorable one at Calais, when Philippa, as described in a familiar chapter of Froissart, obtained pardon for the rich burgesses of the city, who knelt before the irate Edward, clad only in their shirts, with halters about their necks, to save their fellow citizens from destruction.* As Chaucer never tires of saying: "Pity runneth soon in gentle heart."

Of the two lovers of Emelye, the poet evidently portrays Arcite with more favour than Palamon.

> *Half so wel biloved a man as he*
> *Ne was ther never in court, of his degree;*
> *He was so gentil of condicioun,*
> *That thurghout al the court was his renoun.*

Arcite is almost quixotically generous. The most striking example of his sense of honour is where he refuses to take any advantage of his ferocious rival, who had just denounced him as a false, wicked traitor, his mortal foe, and threatened him with death.

Arcite, being armed, could have slain Palamon instantly. Instead, he shows great self-control, acknowledges his opponent a worthy knight, and offers
him a chance to "darreyne" Emelye in open battle.
His generosity goes farther. He undertakes to bring
food and drink and bedding secretly to Palamon,
to strengthen him for the encounter. He will also
provide armour for both, begging his opponent to
choose the best and leave the worst for him. On this
he gives his word as a knight; yet he realizes that his
courtesy may cost him—as in the end it does—both
his lady and his life. This is one of the earliest instances in English literature of what we call "fair
play." The ideal of fair play arose as a guide to knights
in martial encounter, "in battle or in tournament."

Plainly, the chief part of Chaucer's tale is the
account of the tournament. Everything leads up to
this; everything depends on its result. In this part
of the story the poet varies in all but general features
from his source. The Knight's Tale might almost be
called the Tale of the Tournament. In like manner,
Edward III might almost be called the King of the
Tournament. The number of jousts that he held was
legion, and their magnificence was unparalleled in
English history. Even a cursory examination shows
that Chaucer's tournament is astonishingly like those
of Edward III, while quite impossible for Theseus
in Athens.

For trusteth wel, that dukes, erles, kinges,
Were gadered in this noble companye,
For love and for encrees of chivalrye.

After having enumerated the armour that the combatants wore (most of it of quite recent contrivance), the poet, seeing the humour of the anachronisms, remarked slyly: "There is no new guise that is not old." Well aware of what he was doing,* and with deliberate intent of arousing greater interest by making his characters as much as possible like those whom his readers knew, he so altered the *mise en scène* as to give us a valuable picture of the outer chivalry of his own time, substantiated as true by all sorts of evidence.

The moral discourse, moreover, at the end of the tale, on the text, "The king must die as well as the page," is in curious accord with the sentiments of the poem composed in French by the Black Prince to be placed on his tomb. And the memorable speech which follows, in which Theseus declares that it is very much better for a knight to die in his excellence and flower "than when his name has grown pale by age" and "all forgotten is his vassalage," might have been uttered by the ghost of Edward III delivering a warning. In any case, it offered the only consolation the people had for the death of the Black Prince; and of the Black Prince, *preud'omme et en faits et en dits, la fleur de chevalerie, le prince qui ot cœr* *gentil,** one cannot fail to think in connection with Arcite. Chaucer is realistic in his presentation of the life of chivalry in the Knight's Tale.

Was he realistic also, we wonder, in the tale of Sir Thopas? That "rhyme" has sometimes been grotesquely misunderstood. It was not intended, of course, to ridicule romance in general, but only the degenerate versions of courtly poems prepared for ignorant audiences in England, written in a metre never employed on the Continent for the same purpose, and wholly unsuited to extended narrative— "drasty rhyming," without appeal. It was, of course, still less intended to ridicule chivalry in general. But Chaucer told this "tale of mirth" himself, and we suspect that he was up to something more pointed in it than a mere parody of "Horn Child and of Ypotys, of Bevis and Sir Guy." Flanders in the fourteenth century was the actual home of many a fantastic chevalier, noted more for his "fair bearing" than his might, more concerned with "paramours and jollity" than genuine war, decked out gorgeously, but white-faced, and easily-wearied "for pricking on the soft grass."

The tale of Sir Thopas is certainly a "dainty thing." Chaucer seems in it to be poking fun at contemporary affectations, in a mood not unlike that of Shakespeare in *Love's Labour's Lost*. He often laughs at "colours of rhetoric," "art poetical," all pretentious "high style." We may feel confident that he admired no more than Hotspur a popinjay knight. While recent investigations have shown that chivalric customs in Flanders in Chaucer's day were particularly susceptible to mockery, there were also many so-called knights in England who counterfeited valiant heroes of the time and type of the Black Prince, as an ape, or "as craft counterfeiteth kind." For such Chaucer had no respect.

One should note particularly that the only person who is mentioned in the Prologue as an attendant of the Knight and Squire was a Yeoman. The poet was evidently proud of this Yeoman, whom he describes sympathetically in his green suit, with peacock arrows at his girdle, with a mighty bow in his hand. And he might well have been! The English archer-yeomen were the real victors at Crécy and Poictiers. The French nobility in their self-confidence disdained the support of unhorsed warriors; the English welcomed them to their cause, and fought willingly at their head. It was very English of Chaucer to introduce the Yeoman in this way. If it was might of the commons, as Langland said, that made the king reign, it was might of the yeomen that made the knights win. Chivalry in England, the commons believed, should justify itself to gain their support. Chivalry in England was democratized, and it therefore lived.

V

So far we have looked chiefly at mature warriors and
tales of "arms." It is time now to consider another
representative pilgrim who figures forth in prospect,
not so much the body as the soul of chivalry, its first
animating impulse, love.

No one questions the charm of Chaucer's Squire,
a most engaging youth. He was wonderfully quick
and of great strength, a good horseman, a good
jouster, a good dancer. Though but twenty years of
age, he had already borne himself well in military
expeditions. "He could make songs and well endite."
He promised to be peerless in eloquence.

> *Curteys he was, lowly, and servisable,*
> *And carf biforn his fader at the table.*

His gentle, feeling speech, and his discretion won
the heart of the Franklin, who could not help contrasting him with his own son, a waster and wanton,
who paid no heed to virtue. The Host also approved
of the Squire, to judge from the respectful way in
which he invited him to tell his tale. And, indeed,
the friendliness, the modesty, the "good-will" which
the young man showed in doing his part for the
general entertainment, must have made him beloved
by all. The Squire had evidently taken to heart the
idealistic precepts of the order of chivalry, which
he was later to adorn. "Sire," said Prince Huon of

Tabary, in explaining to Saladin, his conqueror, the significance of a knight's baptism, resembling that of a child:

> *Sire, tout ensement devez*
> *Issir sans nule vilonnie,*
> *Et estre plains de courtoisie;*
> *Baignier devez en honeste,*
> *En courtoisie et en bonte,*
> *Et fere amer a toutes genz.**

To this end—that of being worthy of all men's love—an aspiring, chivalric youth was encouraged to seek straightway the love of a particular lady. The Squire had shown his prowess in war, "in hope to stand well in his lady's grace." He was "a lover and a lusty bachelor." Many similar figures meet us in the pages of Froissart as actual combatants of the period, but perhaps none is more conspicuous than Sir Walter Manny, Knight of the Garter, who died in 1372. As a youth he had accompanied Queen Philippa when she left Valenciennes for London to be crowned. "At that time," we read, "were great jousts, tourneys, dancing, carolling, and great feasts every day, the which endured the space of three weeks." After they were ended, most of the bride's company returned, but Walter Manny "abode still with the queen, and was her carver, and after did many great prowesses in divers places." "Let me never be beloved with my lady, unless I have a course with one of these followers," he once ex-

claimed before a combat in Brittany, and sallied forth
to do "noble deeds." Whereupon the countess on
whose behalf he had fought, " descended down from
the castle with a glad cheer and came and kissed
Sir Walter Manny and his companions one after
another two or three times, like a valiant lady."

> *Des femes venent les proesces*
> *Et les honours et les hautesces,*
> *Qui de femes s'est fait haier*
> *Jà ne verrés bien acheveir.*

So we read in a most interesting poem, entitled *Les
Enseignements d'Edouard III*, in which a prince is
instructed how to be a *preud'omme*.* " A knight may
never be of prowess but if he be a lover"—Sir Tristram's words in the *Morte d'Arthur*—express general chivalric belief.

In the *Legend of Good Women*, Chaucer informs
us (through the lips of Alceste) that "while he was
young," he "kept Love's estate," served him with
his cunning, and furthered his law in verse. Like
the hero of his *Book of the Duchess*, the poet chose
love for his "first craft." He might just as well have
learned "other art or letter," but he was impress-
ionable like a white wall, and poems of love came
to him, it seemed, by nature. Therefore, he kept
on in this way, writing "books, songs, ditties," in
praise of love. The poet had made his head ache,
he tells us, many a night, writing in his study

about "Love's folk," furthering, not despising them; though he was not among those whom Love cared to advance.

Chaucer refers more than once to his own experiences of love, but that we cannot take his statements literally is, of course, clear. It is noteworthy that in describing his own lovesickness he uses the same extravagant phrases that the characters of his stories do: he cannot sleep; he has no feeling in anything; he is in dread to die; he is distraught with fantasies; and this sickness has lasted for eight years. All French poets of the period seem to have had similar experiences, and led a "cruel life unsoft."

There is no question that Chaucer knew well the ways of courtly lovers. He gives us interesting sidelights on them in the *House of Fame*, even alluding to the peculiar vows that it was then the chivalrous custom to make.* But Chaucer, always extremely sensitive to insincerity, and always alive to the ridiculous, always (good practical Englishman that he was) a believer in common sense, sedulously avoided the rhetorical excesses of the love poets of his age. "Why," he asks, "should I speak more quaintly, or pain myself to paint my words to speak of love? It will not be. I can naught of that faculty." Very seldom indeed did Chaucer write fantastic verse. "I do," he says, "no diligence to show craft, but only sentence [sense]." In like manner, there is nothing "crafty" or artificial, let alone deceitful or transient, in the chivalrous love that Chaucer commends.

More and more, as time went on, the poet seems to have refrained from association with "lovers." The eagle in the *House of Fame* complains that he took no more interest in "tidings of love and such glad things." Good Alceste thought he might be a renegade, and the god of love even accused him of making wise folk withdraw from him, holding "that he is only a very proper fool who loves paramours too hard and hot." Yet Chaucer maintained that he always desired to speak well of love. Though he did not wish to be a lover, though he did not take sides with the leaf or the flower (alluding to certain love societies of the time), he wrote "in honour of love," and even declares that "no true lover shall come in hell."

The Squire was a pattern lover, and his tale promised to be a pattern tale; but alas! the poet left it "half-told." We have in the prelude a portrait of the noble King Cambinskan of Tartary, who is seen to have all the characteristics of mediaeval distinction, and we have a description of a splendid birthday feast, of just such a sort as the poet may often have enjoyed; but the essential part of the tale as it stands is the experience of a false lover which the beautiful princess Canacee hears from the lips of a bird in distress. The gentle falcon had been chivalrously wooed

by a tercelet who "seemed to be the well of all gentilesse," but he turned out to be a hypocrite, "full
of treason and falseness," and had basely neglected
her for a common bird whom he had met in another
land where he was obliged to go "for his honour."

This poem, animated by the same moral thought as
his *Queen Anelida and False Arcite*, deals veiledly,
it may be, with an actual happening to one whom
Chaucer knew; but that is too long a subject to
broach here. The main thing is the author's exposi-
tion of what must have been one of the greatest diffi-
culties of chivalrous love-service! "Men love by their
very nature newfangleness," says the poet, "and
often no gentleness of blood may them bind." Herein
lay his personal grief; sometimes the word of a born
gentleman was no better than that of men in general; sometimes his love was as low as a churl's.*
Chaucer's address to Tarquinius, the seducer of Lucrece, shows clearly his manner of thought:

> *Tarquinius, that art a kinges eyr,*
> *And sholdest, as by linage and by right,*
> *Doon as a lord and as a verray knight,*
> *Why hastow doon dispyt to chivalrye?*
> *Why hastow doon this lady vilanye?*
> *Allas! of thee this was a vileins dede!*

These lines exhibit his peculiar method of mod-
ernizing the sentiments of ancient story, but still
more his insistence on chivalry as a superior code

of morals. In this respect, as in so many others, he shared the sentiments of his Parson: "Ever from the higher degree that man falleth, the more is he thrall, and more to God and to the world vile and abominable."

Loyalty, the poet felt, was absolutely essential to a lover. At the very mention or thought of a man who proved false, he lost all his customary benignity and flared forth in indignation. No place pleasanter than the nethermost hell was suitable for such an one's eternal abode. The consoling sentiment that is expressed nowadays by the proverb: "There are as good fish in the sea as ever were caught," which corresponds to the one quoted in the *Parliament of Fowls:* "There are more stars, God knows, than a pair," Chaucer describes as "dung-hill" in character, fit for barnyard fowl, but not for noble birds of the air. The turtle-dove said: "Love till death."* In Chaucer's eyes gentleness implied purity. To him chivalrous love meant idealism in life.

Ideal love, with its concomitant of fidelity to troth, is the theme of one of the most charming of the *Canterbury Tales*, the Breton Lay of the Franklin. Perhaps the close relations between England and Brittany in the poet's time (many an English knight had fought there, and the young Duke and Duchess of Brittany resided in England) gave added interest to the story of a Breton knight who came to England "to seek in arms worship and honour." But Chaucer's choice of the tale and its juxtaposition in the general group are significant as showing the teaching he desired to impress. Though he often dwells wittily, in a clerkly, after-dinner mood, on the temptations of sex, the poet always seems glad to pay tribute, as in the Squire's Tale, to the "truth that is in women seen." Here we have another lady whose colour was true blue. And happily she is wedded to one equal to her in fidelity. The knight Arviragus is "the flower of chivalry"—not merely a "worthy man of arms," but a perfect lover, a devoted servant of his lady, without jealousy, without suspicion—and his wife Dorigen is a mirror of wifely chastity, sad in his absence, joyful on his return. But in her circle was a young squire, of whom no harm is said, save that he had the misfortune to fall in love with this noble wife, and the indiscretion to try to win her love in return. This squire Aurelius is painted sympathetically, like the Squire in the Prologue. But he was young, poetic, sensitive, and, as became a person of his sort, a "servant of Venus." According to Continental ideas of the "gay science," there was only merit in his devoting himself assiduously to a married lady. Aurelius, however, recognized that it would be "churlish" to keep Dorigen to a promise she had no desire to fulfil. He was so deeply impressed by the sincerity of her love for her husband that he preferred to suffer himself rather than disturb it, and he proclaims her the truest and the best wife he has ever known.

The "great gentilesse" of Arviragus led to the squire's "gentle deed," which in its turn led to a "gentle deed" from the bachelor of law, to whom the squire had plighted his troth. The moral is: gentleness begets gentleness. The whole secret of the inspiration to gentle deeds on the part of every man in the tale—knight, squire, and clerk—was the fidelity of a lady to her plighted word. After reading such a tale as that of the Franklin, our English word "betrothed" renews its mediaeval significance; it implies a chivalric obligation.

The Franklin's gentle story of "perfect wifehood" ends the so-called marriage group in the *Canterbury Tales*, and probably indicates Chaucer's mature conclusion that love in marriage, without mastery on either side, is the sort of love most highly to be approved.*

VI

FOR Chaucer's chief treatment of love, however, we must turn to that marvellously subtle poem *Troilus and Cressida*, the depth and seriousness of which have escaped many readers, who have been over-engrossed by the intrigue of the story, or by the author's masterly portrayal of a humorous character.

Troilus and Cressida is far from being, as some think, a light-hearted narrative of erotic impulse, a comic tale of how a pandar helped a friend to satisfy sensual desires, a cynical exposure of the instability of an amorous woman. It is at bottom an earnest presentation of the circumstances and effects of idealistic passion, a revelation of the way chivalric fidelity may ennoble a gentleman and unchivalric disloyalty bring a lady to scorn, a solemn plea for perfect devotion and inviolable truth in relations of love.

The hero Troilus first appears on the scene with a company of gay young knights and squires, but, unlike them, shows indifference to ladies. "There was not a man of greater hardiness than he, nor more desired worthiness;" he had "excellent prowess;" but he did not hold lovers in reverence; he thought they worshipped Saint Idiot. He was scornful, haughty, and vain. Then suddenly he was overwhelmed by the sight of Cressida, and his whole being changed through "the fire of love."

> Dede were his japes and his crueltee,
> His heighe port and his manere estraunge,
> And ech of tho gan for a vertu chaunge.

In the field against the Greeks, he was like a lion; but in the town his manner was so goodly that "every one loved him that looked on his face." When, after a combat, he returned to the city with his armour smashed and hewn, "and aye the people cried, 'here cometh our joy,'" Troilus cast down his eyes with modesty. All his "thews" were good. He was no boaster—"too wise [was] he to do so great a vice;" he had a humble, true and pitying heart; he was a noble, gentle knight, "as gentle man as any wight in Troy."

It was, however, of the love of Troilus, not of his arms or knighthood, as seen in many a cruel battle, that Chaucer undertook to write. And he pictures Troilus as a perfect lover—humble, true, secret, patient in pain, ever fresh in desire, diligent to serve, and devoted with a good heart. Cressida had no fault to find with him in any way. Her own reason for yielding to him is particularly worthy of note:

> *For trusteth wel, that your estat royal,*
> *Ne veyn delyt, nor only worthinesse*
> *Of you in werre, or torney marcial,*
> *Ne pompe, array, nobley, or eek richesse,*
> *Ne made me to rewe on your distresse;*
> *But* moral virtue, grounded upon trouthe,
> *That was the cause I first hadde on you routhe!*

Instead of "moral virtue, grounded upon truth," Boccaccio had written, "thy lofty and lordly demeanour, thy high spirit and chivalrous talk" — a great and significant difference! Chaucer here secured moral elevation at the expense of consistency in delineating character.

Cressida also the poet portrays with sympathy.

She was angelic in native beauty, with voice melodious, simple, womanly, and wise. "Her goodly looking gladdened all the press;" "never lacked her pity;" she was "gracious to do well," both "of young and old full well beloved." Chaucer did not regard it as a crime in her that she yielded to Troilus. He makes it clear that she knew what she was doing in going to the first meeting with her lover at Pandarus' house. Love had his dwelling "within the subtle streams of her eyes." Troilus had been overcome by it, and she loved in return. But Cressida proved untrue—therein lay her grievous sin. To be unfaithful to one who had done no wrong, who was, as she declared, a "sword of knighthood, source of gentilesse," was an unpardonable offence. As Chaucer portrays her, Cressida had no excuse for her infidelity, and she offers none. Her sorrowful lament at the end is all because she herself lacked truth. Troilus had refused to believe in her weakness as long as he could, and when at last he knew all, he simply said: "Alas! your name of truth is now fordone, and that is all my ruth." It was past his understanding. "'O God!' quoth he, 'that oughtest take heed to further truth.'" The poet was similarly moved, and himself prayed: "Every lover in his truth advance;" "keep them that be true."

In *Troilus* Chaucer is plainly under the influence of the Italians,* pondering, as deeply as his mind allowed, on love as a mystical passion. Inspired by Boccaccio, he wrote with fine phrase:

> *Plesaunce of love, O goodly debonaire,*
> *In gentil hertes ay redy to repaire!*
> *O verray cause of hele and of gladnesse,*
> *Yheried be thy might and thy goodnesse!*

Here we are in the atmosphere of Guido Guinizelli:

> *Within the gentle heart Love shelters him,*
> *As birds within the green shade of the grove.*
> *Before the gentle heart, in Nature's scheme,*
> *Love was not, nor the gentle heart ere Love.*

Love, says the poet, "makes hearts digne." It "makes worthy folk worthier of name, and causeth most to dread vice and shame." All under its influence become courteous and benign. Could it be otherwise, when God is love?

> *God loveth, and to love wol nought werne;*
> *And in this world no lyves creature,*
> *Withouten love, is worth, or may endure.*

Troilus emphasizes the result of Cressida's "benignity" upon him. He feels unworthy, but recognizes that he must amend in some wise, through the virtue of her high service. God, he believed, had created him to love his lady, and he takes her as his "star," his teacher. In the first rapture of accomplished desire, he breaks out in an apostrophe to Venus, in which is mingled part of Dante's final Invocation to Mary:

Benigne love, thou holy bond of thinges,
Whoso wol grace, and list thee nought honouren,
Lo, his desire wol flee withouten winges.

The idea of love as the "holy bond of things"
Chaucer took from Boethius. "Love," said the latter, "holdeth together people joined with an holy
bond, and knitteth sacrament of marriages of chaste
love; and love enditeth laws to true fellows. O! weal-
ful were mankind, if that same love that governeth
heaven governed your courages!" Boethius always
helped to dignify Chaucer's thought.

Troilus is incomparably more uplifted than the
Filostrato, on which it is based. A difference in tone
is manifest throughout the works, but most notably at the end, where Chaucer replaces Boccaccio's
worldly advice: "Control evil appetite; believe not
all women," and the like, by lofty spiritual pleading.
He implores all the young and fresh to turn their
thoughts from worldly vanity to God, and love Him,
who for love died for them.

For He nil falsen no wight, dar I seye,
That wol his herte al hoolly on Him leye.
And sin He best to love is, and most meke,
What nedeth feyned loves for to seke?

Finally, with deep and genuine emotion, he appeals
to the "soothfast Christ" for mercy, begging Jesus,
for the love of His benign mother, to defend him
against visible and invisible foes, and make him

worthy of grace. In this conclusion the poet again followed Dante, but he wrote the plea "with all [his] heart."

There was nothing incongruous in Chaucer's ending *Troilus* with a quotation from the great Italian. He had been stirred by Dante's spirit, and had exalted love in Dante's sense. As an eminent critic has remarked: "The phrase of Dante, 'Love that withdraws my thought from all vile things,' would have been unintelligible to Catullus. This new aspect of love the modern world owed to chivalry, to Christianity, to the Germanic reverence for women, in which religious awe seems to have been blended with the service of the weaker by the stronger." "Dante is the most luminous example in literature of the chivalrous ecstasy of love." *

VII

THERE were some parts of *Troilus and Cressida* which the author knew would not please all "lovers," whose good opinion he desired, particularly that which told "how Troilus came to his lady's grace." He already heard precious folk say: "I would not procure love thus." He calls attention, therefore, to the fact that there were sundry ways of winning love in sundry lands in sundry ages. In love "each country has its laws," he remarks, making clear that the laws of love in Boccaccio's land differed from those

of his own. Though Chaucer had no narrow desire
to judge all foreigners by English standards, there
can be no doubt that he accepted these as his. He
was not intolerant; he was not prudish; but he honoured virtue in women, and approved fidelity in
marriage bonds.

Near the end of *Troilus*, he begs "every gentle
woman" to be not wroth with him because Cressida
was untrue. He was not responsible for her guilt.
He would, he asserts, more gladly write of the truth
of Penelope and good Alceste. Here he was looking
forward to the composition of the *Legend of Good
Women*. In the remarkable prologue to that poem,
he hints that he composed *Troilus* because he was
"bidden of some person" whom he durst not "with-
say," and thus protests his good intent:

> Whatso myn auctour [*Boccaccio*] mente,
> *Algate, God wot, hyt was myn intente,*
> *To forthren trouthe in love and hit cheryse;*
> *And to be war fro falsenesse and fro vyce,*
> *By swich ensample; this was myn meninge.*

Afterwards he puts on Love's lips these reproaches
for himself:

> *Than seyde Love, "a ful gret negligence*
> *Was hit to thee, to write unstedfastnesse*
> *Of woman,* sith thou knowest hir goodnesse
> By preef, *and eek by stories heer-biforn;* . . .
> *For of Alceste shulde thy writyng be,*
> Sin that thou wost that kalendar is she

Of goodnesse, for she taughte of fyn lovinge,
And namely of wyfhood the livinge,
And alle the boundes that she ogte kepe."

In whose likeness Chaucer would have pictured the ideal Alceste, had he reached her legend, we can never be quite sure. But we know that he would have presented her as a very calendar of goodness, a teacher of fine loving, especially in wifehood. Very different was the teaching of the brilliant Countess Marie de Champagne, who inspired Chrétien's *Lancelot, ou le Chevalier de la Charette.* Chaucer had the advantage of knowing the goodness of women "by proof." He knew not only "the good Queen Anne" of Bohemia (wedded to Richard II in 1382), to whom he planned to dedicate the *Legend* when complete, but also— much earlier, longer, and more intimately—the circle of "the good Queen Philippa," whose renown had doubled after her death.

It has been said that one can estimate a writer's character by his heroines. In chivalric poems, where ladies play so large a part, it is peculiarly important to see how they appear. Chaucer, in a way distinctly different from that of Continental romance, represented goodness as necessary to ideal gentlewomen. Noble ladies, he insisted, should be like virtuous Alceste, "womanly, benign and meek." In this respect Chaucer established an English tradition, and saved chivalry in his land from a grave reproach it might otherwise have seemed to merit, that of being an encouragement of frivolity or a cloak for vice.

Chaucer reveals himself constantly as very sensitive to the opinion of gentle folk. He labours the point, when he permits himself to tell a coarse tale, that he is doing it, not because he approves or even likes the story, but because he feels bound to do so in deference to truth. With emphasis he remarks:

> The Miller is a cherl, *ye knowe wel this;*
> *So was the Reve and other many mo.*

And we are left to draw our own conclusions as to ourselves. Do we approve of the matter in the tales of the Miller, the Reeve, and their crowd, then we are of their type: we too are churls at heart!*

Chaucer does not picture any of his pilgrims as squeamish, but there was, he makes clear, a limit to their endurance. The gentles refused to hear the Pardoner tell of ribaldry, but were all ready for "some moral thing," from which they might profit. Accepting their rebuke, that "full vicious man" brazenly prepares to tell a moral tale. The situation was the opposite with the poet. He shows us by himself that, while one may recognize tales to be churlish and best suited to the low-born, one may relate them and still be a full gentle man. Yet we cannot conceive of Chaucer's Knight or Parson doing this under any circumstances. They were ideal figures. The poet would have been the first to acknowledge that he was not so good as they.

Properly, from an aristocratic standpoint, Chaucer should have arranged his personages according to rank. In society the laws of precedence were, and the poet felt should be, strictly observed.* But his pilgrims, for the most part, were not in society, and at any rate artistic effect, he saw, forbade grouping them together. When one stops to think what the *Canterbury Tales* would have been like if Chaucer had followed the plan of "setting folk in their degree," one discovers that the gentles are all dignified, and tell tales becoming to their station—tales of "gentleness, morality, and holiness." Not one of them is in the least coarse in his or her utterance. Half of the clergy are low or wanton; but something, evidently, separates the gentles from such defilement. Without snobbishness, in frank and open fellowship, they associate with the vulgar crowd and preserve their distinction. This effect is very subtly achieved by the poet. He makes his readers feel that "reverence" is due the gentles, because their conduct is without reproach.

Every wight was full blithe and glad when the Knight drew the lot to begin the tales; and when he finished there was no one, young or old (though "especially the gentles every one"), who did not declare his was a "noble story and worthy for to draw in memory." From the beginning to the end of the pilgrimage, while the churls treat each other roughly, while they show contempt for various ecclesiastics among them, they do not utter a disrespectful word to or of a gentle in their midst. They show them spontaneous, willing deference, even the burly Host, though he did not care a straw for the gentilesse of the Franklin, "Epicurus' own son," who was not thoroughbred. Harry Bailey offers a constant, unconscious foil to the gentles' real quality. When the Knight interrupts the Monk's dreary tragedies, he does it with grace and courtesy, as well as good reason. But the atmosphere changes abruptly when the Host, backing him up, undertakes to state his own opinion. His first phrase is characteristically an oath. Already the Parson had rebuked the Host for this manifestation of his coarseness; and later, when he tells his own tale, he dwells upon this sin: "What say we eek of them that delight in swearing, and hold it gentry or manly deed to swear great oaths? And what of them that, of verray usage, cease not to swear great oaths, all be the cause not worth a straw? Certes, this is horrible sin." The Knight and other gentles avoided swearing noticeably. The Prioress's greatest oath was but by St. Loy.

> [*She*] *peyned hir to countrefete chere*
> *Of court, and been estatlich of manere,*
> *And to been holden digne of reverence.*
> *In curteisye was set ful much hir lest.*

VIII

CHAUCER reached maturity at a time of profound social unrest, when crowds of his countrymen were swayed to revolt by the ominous cry:

> *When Adam delved and Eve span,*
> *Where was then the gentleman?*

In contemporary France the followers of Jack Goodman likewise sought with violence to overwhelm the nobility. The poet observed that "the rude people" had "no great insight in virtue," and, in the Clerk's Tale, addressed them with contempt:

> *"O stormy peple! unsad and ever untrewe!*
> *Ay undiscret and changing as a vane,*
> *Delyting ever in rumbel that is newe,*
> *For lyk the mone ay wexe ye and wane;*
> *Your doom is fals, your constance yvel preveth,*
> *A ful greet fool is he that on you leveth!"*

Yet he also averred in the same narrative that "under low degree was often virtue hid," and, whatever his views of the crowd, he had too much human sympathy not to encourage the aspirations of every individual.

> *For God it woot, that children ofte been*
> *Unlyk her worthy eldres hem before;*
> *Bountee comth al of God, nat of the streen*
> *Of which they been engendred and y-bore.*

Even had England enjoyed social tranquillity in his day, Chaucer's thought would inevitably have been

directed to the eternal, universal question of true
gentleness, since sundry of those authors whom he
most admired had occupied themselves with the
problem, and it was congenial for him to consider.
In his early years he read, if no others, the discus-
sions in the *Roman de la Rose,* and later those of
Boethius and Dante.

Guillaume de Lorris, like various French writers
before him, at least as far back as Wace in the
twelfth century, declared that *Vilonie fait li vilains,*
but, aristocrat that he was in his attitude, he carefully avoided even implying the reverse: *Gentilesse
fait li gentilhomme.* He felt that common people had
nothing to do with honour or courtesy.

> *Vilains est fel et sans pitié,*
> *Sans servise et sans amitié.**

Jean de Meung, on the contrary, emphatically asserts: *Nus n'est gentis s'il n'est as vertus ententis;* and
in the long and straightforward examination of the
subject by Nature, which follows, he proclaims the
same democratic doctrine that Chaucer was later to
show forth, though with less defiance and asperity.
Unlike the great satirist by whom he was so much
influenced, Chaucer was a courtier himself; he loved
to associate with gentle folk; and he presented his
views without cynicism or vexation, in a mood of
compromise, void of offence.

In his "moral ballade" entitled *Gentilesse*, the poet asserts that "any one who claims to be gentle must follow virtue and flee vice, for dignity belongeth to virtue, and not the reverse, even in him who wears mitre, crown or diadem." Though he never ceases to applaud gentleness, Chaucer steadily insists that it should not depend on mere outward adherence to conventions, but spring from the heart and stimulate good deeds. Gentleness, he maintains, cannot be passed on, like title or riches, from father to son. It is wholly dependent on an individual's "virtuous noblesse," "that is appropriated to no degree, but to the first Father in majesty."*

The poet's most ample discussion of the subject he puts into the mouth of Dame Ragnell, heroine of the Arthurian tale of the Wife of Bath. Are we gentle, she asks, merely because our elders were? Certainly not! is the definite answer; that is unjustified arrogance. Our parents cannot bequeath their "virtuous living," that made them to be called gentlemen. "Gentry is not annexed to possessions," for, God knows, we often find a lord's son doing shame and villainy. Let a man be born of a gentle house, granted that his elders were noble and virtuous, if he will not himself do gentle deeds, he is not gentle, be he duke or earl. "Villain's sinful deeds make a churl."

> *Loke who that is most vertuous alway,*
> *Privee and apert, and most entendeth ay*

To do the gentil dedes that he can.
And tak him for the grettest gentil man.

Once again we find Chaucer establishing his con-
victions by the example of Boethius and Dante,
to whom, along with Seneca,* he here makes open
reference. The *Purgatorio* of "the wise poet of
Florence" furnished him the lines:

Ful selde up ryseth by his branches smale
Prowesse of man; for God, of his goodnesse,
Wol that of Him we clayme our gentilesse.

But we seem also to hear echoes of the Fourth
Treatise of the *Convivio* when he presents the problem as that of "such gentilesse as is descended out
of old riches." Dante, with Frederick II's views in
mind, repudiates the "false thought" that folk are
gentle "because of race which has long abode in great
wealth." "I affirm," he says, "that nobility in its
constituent essence ever implies the goodness of its
seat as baseness ever implies ill. ... Gentleness is
wherever there is virtue." "He is not only base (that
is ungentle) but the very basest, who is descended
from good forbears but is himself bad."

The same thought is expressed with peculiar
beauty in the *canzone* of Guido Guinizelli, already
referred to, which Dante himself so much admired:

The sun strikes full upon the mud all day;
It remains vile, nor the sun's worth is less.
"By race I am gentle," the proud man doth say:
He is the mud, the sun is gentleness.

> *Let no man predicate*
> *That aught the name of gentleness should have,*
> *Even in a king's estate,*
> *Except the heart there be a gentle man's.*
> *The star-beam lights the wave, —*
> *Heaven holds the star and the star's radiance.**

Happily, Chaucer brooded earnestly upon this theme and perpetuated to us the wisest opinion current in his time.

It would be interesting to review the extensive comment on the subject of nobleness back to antiquity; but there is no need. We find everywhere in the mediaeval conception of "gentilesse," or "gentilezza," an element which is obviously lacking in classical thought, the element of Christian feeling, mystical and sweet. It is more important to note that Chaucer was not alone in England in espousing the cause of virtue as essential to honour. Wycliffe and Gower did the same thing, and Langland wrote these words of advice to a knight:

> *Beguile not thy bondman, the better thou 'lt speed;*
> *Though under thee here, it may happen in Heaven*
> *His seat may be higher, in saintlier bliss,*
> *Than thine, save thou labour to live as thou shouldst,*
> *In the charnel at church, churls are hard to discover,*
> *Or a knight from a knave there; this know in thy heart.**

The tale of the Parson, brother of the Plowman, was planned to "knit up well a great matter," and the Parson's words we may also use in the same way.

It is not without significance that he speaks of the
"gentilesse" of "the courteous Lord Jesu Christ,"
and contrasts it with the "vileinye" of the Devil. He
dwells earnestly on the danger of pride in gentry,
pointing out that "oftentimes the gentry of the body
steals away the gentry of the soul." "Forsooth," he
declares, "one manner of gentry is to be praised,
that which apareleth man's courage with virtues and
moralities and maketh him Christ's child. For trust
well, that over what man sin hath mastery, he is a
very churl to sin." The poet plainly believed that
true gentleness is informed by grace. It comes, he
says, "from God alone."

This study of Chaucer has aimed to bring to view
an important feature of his work which has been
singularly overlooked by most of his critics. If, as
Saint Augustine said, "we estimate a man not by
what he knows, nor by what he believes, but by what
he loves," it must be clear that one of the chief bases
of our judgement of Chaucer henceforth should be
his attitude towards chivalry, since there is nothing,
perhaps, that he loved more. Had Chaucer not written so many poems and tales of gentleness, as well
as of morality and holiness, he would certainly not
have won the reverence of the numerous "sage and
serious" men who have applauded him from his day
to our own.

Chaucer's attitude toward chivalry was pragmatic. He regarded the circumstances of knighthood in his day with common sense. He recognized that there were then, and must be, gentle classes, and he did not expect too much in the way of refinement from the lowly in rank. He saw clearly that men of good lineage were by that very fact more predisposed to gentleness. Nevertheless, he was ready to welcome and applaud this virtue wherever it might appear. He encouraged every man to try to exhibit it in his acts. He believed, as do most of us, that "he is gentle who doth gentle deeds."

The chivalry that the poet exalted was that of his own time; it was also that of his own life; but even as it was the best of his time, so it was the best of his life. And because it was then so beautiful, it is alluring still; because it was then so honest, it is of perpetual good report. It has lived, not as a dream, but as a transfiguration of reality.

MALORY

MALORY

WE now leave the domain of chivalry in life for that of chivalry in romance. Passing thus from reality to unreality, we pass, strangely enough, from a poet to a soldier, and from verse to prose. Turning from Geoffrey Chaucer in the fourteenth century to Sir Thomas Malory in the fifteenth, we take a step backward instead of forward, and occupy ourselves with literature of a type almost outworn, animated by exclusive aristocratic sentiment.

Apart from the language, and in so far as it is only what it purports to be, a narrative of knightly adventure, the *Morte d'Arthur* might almost as well have been written seventy years before Chaucer's birth as seventy years after his death. Yet inquiry shows that "this noble and joyous book" is more than a simple "reduction" of early French romance, as is generally believed. "Notwithstanding it treateth of the birth, life, and acts of King Arthur, of his noble knights of the Round Table, their marvellous quests and adventures, the achieving of the Sangreal, and in the end the dolorous death and departing out of this world of them all,"—it was evidently called forth by the author's anxiety regarding conditions in England in his own day, and was intended to be influential for good and not merely entertaining then.

Malory makes no effort to conceal the fact that

he wrote primarily for the gentle-born. "I pray you all, gentlemen and gentlewomen, that read this book of Arthur and his knights from the beginning to the ending"—thus he addresses his friends when about to lay down his pen. Throughout his work he had taken no thought of any other audience, and he finally appeals only to gentlemen and gentlewomen for their prayers after he is dead. Caxton, moreover, states with emphasis who "came and demanded" him to print the book—"many noble and divers gentlemen of this realm of England." He hints, to be sure, that the narrative might appeal to other estates and be pleasant for them to read in; but he insists on the station of those to whom he humbly submits the finished volume. "This said book," he says, "I direct unto all noble princes, lords and ladies, gentlemen or gentlewomen." "This said book" is one of the first ever dedicated in England to Gentle Readers, and Caxton's words have a literal significance that soon became attenuated in frequent use.

In many ways the *Morte d'Arthur* must have interested Malory's contemporaries more than it does us. All of the fifteenth century would recognize in it much more clearly than we a true guide for gentlemen's careers; they could understand better the mode of battle and tourney, whereby heroes still won renown; they could hardly fail to be aroused by seeming parallels in the Arthurian past to the events of

their own present, which have concerned men little
since. On the other hand, we are no doubt attracted
to the work by a certain quaintness of style that only
the passing of years could produce; and the charm of
"far-off, bygone things" in romance, picturing a life
which we have now no duty to mend, draws us with
unalloyed winsomeness as it could not possibly have
done those who felt bound to consider the results
of that life when actually devoid of inspiration and
vitality. Above all, we see the book in a better per-
spective from the point of view of art.

The art of Malory's work an injudicious reader,
even to-day, is apt to overlook. The writing seems
all so natural and simple, so lacking in rhetorical
ornament, that one who is unobservant may readily
be deluded into thinking that little praise is due the
author. But let him compare the *Morte d'Arthur*
with any other work of the same kind, ancient or
modern, let him attempt to improve on any good
passage that attracts him, and he will surely discover
that here is art that conceals art, here is distinction
that, forgetting itself, evades remark.

Malory's book has been reproached with lack of
unity, not altogether without cause. Whoever reads
it as a whole, is certain to be bewildered by the
complexities of certain stories, and by the way the
numerous adventures in a single tale sometimes follow one another in strange confusion. He will dis-

cover also curious inconsistencies in the presentation of character, and contradictions of tone and
sentiment. These faults, however, inhered, and were
much more manifest, in the sources of the book, and
no one can study Malory's methods of composition
in connection with those of his predecessors without great admiration for the skill with which he has
welded together, and stamped with a peculiar personal impress, the vast, incongruous body of material which he undertook to mould.

The *Morte d'Arthur* is the fountain-head of Arthurian fiction, so far as most Englishmen of to-day are
aware; for the many French and Middle-English
documents concerning knights of the Round Table
which were current in mediaeval times are now familiar to none but the scholarly few. Malory, more than
anyone else, deserves the credit of making modern
Englishmen feel that Arthur and his comrades were
national heroes. No doubt this had been the tend-
ency of English writers of the alliterative school from
the poet Layamon at the beginning of the thirteenth
century on; but the great majority among us have
never heard mention of these writers of the rural
west, let alone attempted to read their artless lines.
Save the *Morte d'Arthur*, there was no English book
on the same theme widely read until Tennyson pro-
duced his *Idylls of the King;* and had it not been
for Malory, Tennyson would never have thought

of composing these. To English poets, in fact, the *Morte d'Arthur* has ever seemed a palace of manifold dreams. From it one after another of them has emerged greatly enamoured of old romance, eager to perpetuate the aspirations that it reveals and evokes. After Malory,

> *The mightiest chiefs of English song*
> *Scorned not such legends to prolong.*

It was a prejudiced pedant, Roger Ascham, who in the sixteenth century uttered strong condemnation of the *Morte d'Arthur*, which, he asserted, was "received into the prince's chamber," when "God's Bible was banished the court." "The whole pleasure of [it]," he said, "standeth in open manslaughter and bold bawdry—in which book those be counted the noblest knights that do kill most men without any quarrel, and commit the foulest adulteries by subtlest shifts." Ascham far overshot the mark at which he aimed. To be, like him, a hater of "papistry" did not really necessitate, as he seemed to think, hatred of everything mediaeval—certainly not of chivalry and the "matter of Britain," the chief if not the whole pleasure of which really consists in its potent stimulus to idealistic endeavour. Milton, though a Puritan, had better judgement, along with finer poetic vision. How willingly his imagination played about the scenes of Malory's, as well as of

Spenser's, work! We did not need to have him tell us "whither [his] younger feet wandered;" but still we are glad to have had him frankly state: "I betook me among those lofty fables and romances, which recounted in solemn cantos the deeds of knighthood founded by our victorious kings, and from thence had in renown over all Christendom;"* and while we may be far from thinking him unwise to have chosen a "higher argument" for his mature pen, we cannot but long for that wonderful poem which we should now possess if he had fulfilled his first desire and sung "the great-hearted heroes of the unvanquished Table in their bonds of fellowship." But an epic of Arthur, Milton in the end did not see fit to write; and the *Morte d'Arthur* remains still, probably will always remain, that English work which most nearly merits so lofty a name.

I

IT is only a few years since the author of the *Morte d'Arthur* was identified with reasonable certainty. Century after century had passed, and his work had been continuously enjoyed; but fortune reserved for an American, Professor Kittredge, the pleasure of discovering who the actual Sir Thomas Malory was. Now all seem agreed that he was a knight of ancient family, resident at Newbold Revell (or Fenny Newbold) in Warwickshire. His father, Sir John Malory,

appears to have died in 1434, when Sir Thomas succeeded to the ancestral estates. In 1445 Sir Thomas
represented his county in Parliament. He fought on
the Lancastrian side in the Wars of the Roses, and
apparently very conspicuously, for he was excluded,
along with certain others, from the operation of a
pardon issued by Edward IV in 1468. He died soon
after, on March 14, 1471, probably over seventy years
of age, and was buried, with the superscription *valens
miles*, in the chapel of St. Francis at Grey Friars, in
the suburbs of London. He left a widow, Elizabeth
Malory, who lived until 1480, and a grandson, Nich-
olas, about four years of age. The *Morte d'Arthur*
was finished by Caxton on the last day of July, 1485.

Apart from one important fact, this is all that
we know definitely of our author's biography. But
we can safely surmise a good deal with regard to his
occupations in youth, and conjecture as to some of
his doings later.

Sir John Malory was "sheriff of Leicestershire,
Escheator, Knight of the Shire in the Parliament
of 1413, and held other offices of trust."* By him
Thomas Malory's thoughts were likely to be directed
to the grave problems then troubling the nation.
The many unhappy events which darkened England in the early years of the fifteenth century had
abundantly justified Froissart's anxious foreboding.
There had been serious wars and rumours of wars in

the land. But at last, in 1413, Henry V ascended the throne, and straightway began to rule with vigour. Led by personal ambition, he presently renewed Edward's claim to the throne of France, and crossed the water with his troops. The great unexpected victory of Agincourt in 1415, so terrible a misfortune to the French nobility, delighted the English nation, and made Henry secure in his English, if not in his French, throne.

It is now that Thomas Malory himself first appears on the scene in history — a youth, we presume, of some twenty years, in the military retinue of the famous Richard Beauchamp, Earl of Warwick. This is the important fact in his biography to which reference has already been made. In 1415 Warwick indented to serve the king as Captain of Calais, and "to have with him in time of truce or peace, for the safeguard thereof, thirty men-at-arms, himself and three knights accounted as part of that number; thirty archers on horseback, two hundred archers, all of his own retinue ... and in time of war, he to have one hundred and fifty men on horseback." Thomas Malory, in his retinue, had one lance and two archers, receiving for his lance and one archer twenty pounds per annum and their diet, and for the other archer ten marks and no diet.

"The service of Malory with Richard of Warwick is peculiarly significant in view of the well-known character of the Earl. No better school for the future author of the *Morte d'Arthur* can be imagined than a personal acquaintance with that Englishman whom all Europe recognized as embodying the knightly ideal of the age. The Emperor Sigismund, we are informed on excellent authority, said to Henry V 'that no prince Christian, for wisdom, nurture and manhood, had such another knight as he had of the Earl Warwick;' adding thereto that if all courtesy were lost, yet might it be found again in him; and so ever after, by the emperor's authority, he was called the Father of Courtesy."

In an almost contemporary history of Warwick's life,* from which the emperor's remark is taken, Warwick is presented very much as a knight of the Round Table, and has romantic adventures which make him seem akin to Sir Gareth, one of Malory's favourite heroes. On a certain occasion, when he was Captain of Calais, "casting in his mind to do some new point of chivalry," he appeared at a great tourney on three successive days, unknown, in different armour, and, showing great prowess each time, won much honour. On the third day, we read, the earl "came in face open . . . and said like as he had in his own person performed the two days before, so with God's grace he would the third. Then ran he to the chevalier named Sir Colard Fymes, and every stroke he bare him backward to his horse's back. And then the

Frenchman said he was bound to his saddle, wherefore he alighted down from his horse, and forthwith
stepped up into his saddle again, and so with worship rode to his pavilion, and sent to Sir Colard a
good courser, and feasted all the people, . . . and rode
to Calais with great worship."

This adventure appears to have taken place in
1417, when Thomas Malory, so far as we know, was
still in Warwick's retinue; but we cannot tell exactly
how long he continued a follower of this brilliant
knight, who died in 1439. Probably he was with him
at the famous siege of Rouen in 1419, and at the
marriage of Henry V with Catherine of France the
year after. Whether or no he accompanied Warwick
long on the Continent, he must have heard with special interest of the earl's spectacular achievements
in Italy and the Holy Land.* Since he followed a
knightly career, Malory doubtless participated in the
closing events of the Hundred Years' War. In 1429
Orléans was relieved by Joan of Arc. It would be
interesting to know what so upright a man thought
of that chivalrous maid and of the manner of her
death.

Malory's life embraced the whole turbulent period
of Henry VI's career. The reign of this weak monarch is one of the most unhappy in English history,
not only because of disasters and disgraces abroad,
but more perhaps because of the ceaseless turmoil

of the nobility at home and the lack of any superior power to keep them in control. What part Malory played in these sorry conflicts we are not in a position to say, and inquiry is futile. Apart from warfare, however, there are many questions we should like to ask—especially about the author's friends.

Was he personally acquainted with Prince Charles d'Orléans, a prisoner in London for twenty-five years after the battle of Agincourt, writing in captivity his refined but fragile lyric verse? Or with that other royal captive, King James I of Scotland, so long in the Tower, whiling away his time by the composition of the charming *King's Quair*, a pendant to the Knight's Tale of Chaucer, his master in poetic art? Did he associate with that eminent Lancastrian, Sir John Fortescue, who, devotedly loyal to his party until he saw their cause was hopelessly lost,* finally recanted his political opinions, and lived to write, among other things, an important work on the *Governance of England*, in which he revealed ardent patriotism and an eager desire to help to heal the wounds of his afflicted nation? Was he familiar with the works of Alain Chartier, Christine de Pisan, the Chevalier de la Tour Landry, Antoine de la Sale, or the chivalrous writers of the court of Burgundy? In January, 1430, the Order of the Golden Fleece was founded by Philip the Good, and dedicated to the Virgin and St. Andrew. It was composed of twenty-four members (not including the sovereign), who were expected to be *gentilshommes de nom et d'armes et sans reproche.* Did Malory enjoy intercourse with any of these nobles, who were solemnly pledged to protect Holy Church and uphold virtue throughout life? There is nothing but silence in answer to such questionings!

Professor Kittredge remarked that Malory may have been relieved from the sentence of Edward IV in 1468 by a special pardon, or by the general amnesty of 1469, "since on his death soon after, there seems to have been no question as to the inheritance of his estate." This, however, was only a conjecture, and others have suggested that his burial in Grey Friars may indicate that he died a prisoner in Newgate, near by. At all events, we have good reason to believe that he was actually in prison when he wrote his book, and that when he prayed at the end for "*good deliverance alive,*" he was in danger of death by sickness of the flesh. In support of this view, the following passage, introduced by Malory in the course of his narrative, is significant: "So Sir Tristram endured there great pain, for sickness had undertaken him, and that is the greatest pain a prisoner may have. For all the while a prisoner may have his health of body, he may endure under the mercy of God, and *in hope of good deliverance;* but when sickness toucheth a prisoner's body, then may a prisoner say all wealth is him bereft, and then he hath cause to wail and weep."*

Thomas à Kempis died in the same year as Sir Thomas Malory. The *Imitation of Christ* was widely known in England during the latter's lifetime. If Malory read it, he did so, we may be sure, with full understanding and sympathy. He subscribes himself at the close of his work, "a servant of Jesu by day and night." In the *Imitation* and the *Morte d'Arthur* we view the departing splendour of the Middle Ages— a magnificent afterglow.

> *For though the day be never so long,*
> *At last the bell ringeth to evensong.*

II

WHEN one considers the circumstances of Malory's life—his aristocratic lineage and profession of arms, his training as a gentleman and a soldier, his experience of foreign and civil war, the vicissitudes of his own fortunes, and finally, the fact that he wrote late in life, probably suffering in prison, approaching death —one understands better why the *Morte d'Arthur* is what it is: a work of retrospect, tinged with sadness for the passing of the good old days; a work of idealism, troubled with knowledge of miserable facts daily divulged; a work of patriotism, written when the land was being wasted by civil strife; a work of encouragement to the right-minded, and of warning to the evil-minded, among men of that class in which the author lived and moved.

Malory wrote no preface to his book. Only inci-
dentally does he himself reveal its serious aim, though
now and then he becomes frankly hortatory; but the
worthy Caxton plainly states what decided him to
perpetuate the narrative in type. "Under the favour
and correction of all noble lords and gentlemen," he
"emprised to imprint" the book, "*to the intent* that
noble men may see and learn the noble acts of chivalry, the gentle and virtuous deeds that some knights
used in those days, by which they came to honour,
and how they that were vicious were punished and
oft put to shame and rebuke; humbly beseeching all
noble lords and ladies, with all other estates, of what
estate or degree they be of, that shall see and read in
this said book and work, that they take the good and
honest acts in their remembrance and to follow the
same. Wherein they shall find many joyous and pleasant histories, and noble and renowned acts of humanity, gentleness and chivalry. For herein may be
seen noble chivalry, courtesy, humanity, friendliness,
hardiness, love, friendship, cowardice, murder, hate,
virtue, and sin. Do after the good and leave the evil,
and it shall bring you to good fame and renown. And
for to pass the time, this book shall be pleasant to
read in, but for to give faith and belief that all is true
that is contained therein, ye be at your liberty ; but
all is written for our doctrine, and for to beware that
we fall not to vice and sin, but to exercise and fol-

low virtue, by the which we may come and attain
to good fame and renown in this life, and after this
short and transitory life to come unto everlasting
bliss in Heaven: the which He grant us that reigneth
in Heaven, the blessed Trinity, Amen!"

The *Morte d'Arthur*, Caxton makes clear, was in
his opinion a book of moral edification, as well as one
of entertainment, primarily appealing to the aristocracy of the "noble realm" in which he lived. He
further exalts the work as patriotic in effect. Englishmen, he declares, were to be reproached because foreigners knew more than they of King Arthur, "which
ought most to be remembered amongst us Englishmen, considering that he was a man from within this
realm and king and emperor of the same," — "the
most renowned Christian king, first and chief of
the three best Christians and worthy" — a king "to
whom none earthly prince may compare," who in his
time had "the flower of chivalry of the world with
him" — *rex quondam, rexque futurus.*

Many scholars have concerned themselves with
the mythical conception of Arthur as a resident of
the Otherworld, some time to return to liberate his
British folk; but few, if any, have observed that
Malory's presentation of this ideal monarch was
planned to arouse definite contemporaneous interest
by the subtle enforcing of similitude between past
and present happenings.

"It befell in the days of Uther Pendragon, when
he was king of all England, and so reigned"—these,
Malory's opening words, are notable for their definite
contradiction of the facts of romance on behalf of
the romance of facts. "It befell," like the "once upon
a time" of a fairy tale, immediately transports us
into the realm of remoteness and fable, and "the
days of Uther Pendragon" prepares us to hear tales
of the mighty Celtic warriors whom Geoffrey of
Monmouth created in glorification of ancient Britain. Yet soon we discover that it is with a king of
England we have to do. Malory begins his book as
if he were writing about a monarch of the House of
Lancaster, whose right to the throne was not quite
clear—a king "the which had great war in his days
for to get all England into his hand." "All the battles that were done in Arthur's days," from the ini-
tial one at St. Albans, have a striking resemblance to
those of fifteenth-century England. The first undertakings of the monarch are to defeat his enemies
and establish his kingdom; he has a private counsel-
lor; he appeals to the Archbishop of Canterbury; he
consults his lords and commons; he holds parlia-
ments; his object is the dignity of the nation. Malory
strongly emphasized the idea that Arthur was an
English king; and we see him make alliances, use
strategy, prepare for and carry on war, in the same
spirit, and often in the same places, as the English

of his day. "All men of worship said it was merry to be under such a chieftain that would put his person in adventure as other poor knights did."

One example from near the close of the story must suffice at this time to illustrate the situation.

The king and his followers are off waging a fierce war against the French, "burning and wasting all that they might overrun," for, though we should never have dreamed it before, we are suddenly advised by Malory in his twentieth book, that "to say the sooth Sir Launcelot and his brethren were lords of all France," and it is stated how the various provinces were divided among them. Arthur has left Modred as governor of the kingdom in his absence; but this traitor has taken advantage of his position, cajoled the people, and usurped the throne. He tries to win Guinevere to his wife, but she escapes to the Tower of London, and there defends herself, even against the "cannons" he fires at the walls. Arthur speedily returns, and a great conflict is imminent, when he and Modred compromise on the question of the throne. Arthur is to reign as long as he lives, but Modred is to succeed him.

No one in Malory's time could overlook the similarity of this course of events to contemporary history. Here, however, the author departs from his habitual reserve to make a comparison. "Lo, ye, all Englishmen!" he exclaims; "see ye not what a mischief here was, for he that was the most king and knight of the world, and most loved the fellowship of noble knights, and by him they were all upholden. Now might not these Englishmen hold us [them!] content with him. Lo! thus was the old custom and usage of this land. And also men say that we of this land have not yet lost or forgotten that custom and usage. Alas! this is a great default of all Englishmen, for there may no thing please us no term. And so fared the people at that time; they were better pleased with Sir Modred than they were with King Arthur, and much people drew unto Sir Modred, and said that they would abide with him for better and for worse. And so Sir Modred drew with a great host to Dover, for there he heard say that Sir Arthur would arrive, and so he thought to beat his own father from his lands. And the most party of all England held with Sir Modred, the people were so newfangle."

A little later, when preparations are being made for the last great battle, Malory states: "Then Sir Modred araised much people about London, for they of Kent, Sussex and Surrey, Essex and Suffolk and of Norfolk, held the most party with Sir Modred." It is worth consideration that these were the counties from which Edward of York largely recruited his followers.*

Malory persistently identifies romantic places with English localities. "The city of Camelot," he notes, "is called in English, Westminster." We read of "a town called Astolat, that is now in English Guild-ford;" of "a castle that is called Magouns and now it is called Arundel, in Sussex;" and of Joyous Gard, where Launcelot lived with Guinevere, "some men say it was Alnwick and some say it was Bambor-ough." But the assertion that "the country of Logres" is "the country of England" gives us his chief guid-ing thread. In writing of Arthur and his wars with his nobles, Malory's thoughts were not far from his own land in his own days. "Alas!" we can hear him say like Sir Launcelot: "Alas! that ever I should live to hear that most noble king [Arthur or Henry VI], that made me knight, thus to be overset with his subjects in his own realm." Yet "it is an old said saw, there is hard battle there as kin and friends do battle either against other; there may be no mercy but mortal war." More than once Malory recorded a truth which the world, despite so much experience, never seems to learn: "Better is peace than ever war."

Here he is at one with his sympathetic contempo-rary, Occleve, who near the close of his *De Regimine Principum* makes a strong statement of the woes of "inward war" in England and France in his days, and pleads with touching earnestness for "the gift of peace, that precious jewel." To make war on the miscreants and bring them to the true faith might be meritorious, but "the great dissension, the piteous

harm, the hateful discord" between the Christian
lands, England and France, was a grievous offence to
"the author of concord, the Lord of all realms." This
was particularly sad in his eyes because the "style of
worthiness" of these lands "is rung throughout the
world in all the provinces." Wherefore he urged:
"Give them example; ye be their mirrors; they follow
you." *Mutatis mutandis*, there is something terribly
modern in the situation; and perhaps the cause of our
own twentieth-century anxieties is the same as that in
Occleve's time. "Ambition and covetousness, fire all
this debate." "The kiss of Judas is now widespread."

In the reign of Henry IV, Occleve wrote:

To seek stories old
No need is, since this day sharp war and hard
Is at the door, as men may behold.

He therefore spoke plainly; but Malory was led to
composition somewhat later, under other circumstances, in a different mood. By good fortune he
saw fit to seek old stories, the better to attract his
land to sober thought.

III

NEVER has England had an aristocracy more proud
and privileged, nor, it would seem, more corrupt,
than in the fifteenth century. Unless all contemporary records deceive, some of the most conspicuous
nobles then were reckless, dishonest, sensual, and

brutal, to a degree that we nowadays find hard to believe. Unbridled selfishness and insolence had a natural issue in riot and disorder. Robbery and rape, sacrilege, murder—every sort of foul crime by so-called gentlemen—is openly chronicled. Suspicion and uncertainty afflicted the nation.

To be sure, Commines, a contemporary historian, pays England this tribute: "Now, in my opinion, among all the kingdoms of the world with which I am acquainted, that one where public affairs are best treated, where the people suffer least violence, is England; and there ill-luck and misfortune fall on those who make war." England was certainly no worse than France at the same time. In England, however, as Commines observed with his usual acuteness, the nobles who made war were those to suffer from it, not only in life and fortune, but also—which is more important for us now—in moral strength.

Even as, in his account of Arthur's wars, Malory endeavoured to establish pride in united England, and to show the calamity of wavering truth and allegiance, so also, in the portrayal of good and bad knights, he tried to promote the virtue of individual aristocrats, by whose example society might be improved.

King Arthur he pictures as straightforward and frank, with "a great eager heart," ready to put his own body into jeopardy when need called, bountiful in gifts, generous in praise, forgiving of offence, whom "never yet man could prove untrue to his promise." He "had liefer to die with honour than to live with shame."

Here is the code of honour which the king required of his knights: "Never to do outrage, or murder, and always to flee treason, also by no means to be cruel, but to give mercy unto him that asketh mercy; and also to do to ladies, damsels and gentle women succour upon pain of death—also, that no man take no battles in a wrongful quarrel for no law, nor for the world's goods." "For ever," said Arthur, "it is a worshipful knight's deed to help another worshipful knight when he seeth him in a great danger, for ever a worshipful man will be loth to see a worshipful shamed, and he that is of no worship, and fareth with cowardice, never shall he show gentleness, nor no manner of goodness, where he seeth a man in any danger, for then ever will a coward show no mercy, and *always a good man will do ever to another man as he would be done to himself.* . . . He that was courteous, true, and faithful to his friend, was that time cherished." "All men of worship hate an envious man and will show him no favour. And he that is courteous, kind and gentle, hath favour in every place."

King Mark of Cornwall is portrayed as Arthur's absolute opposite. Mark is repeatedly spoken of as the

most villainous knight (or king) in the world, whose
fellowship all good knights eschewed. He is mean,
wily, and ill-conditioned, a vile recreant, "a fair
speaker and false thereunder," a liar, a traitor, and a
murderer. All knights deem him "the most horrible
coward that ever bestrode a horse."

Though Arthur's presence is always felt in the
background, when he is not conspicuously in the fore-
ground, of the scenes pictured by Malory, the *Morte
d'Arthur* is chiefly occupied with the exploits of
other members of the Round Table brotherhood,
especially of Sir Tristram and Sir Launcelot. Malory
did not invent any new episodes, and the exploits of
his leading heroes have in general a great sameness,
as they had in Old French prose romance. Through
conventional feats of arms, the various knights reveal
one after another whether they are worthy or unworthy of the high standards of their order; and what
those standards were, we have already seen.

Malory discloses the principles of knighthood in-
cidentally, in the course of engaging narrative, but
if one prefers to have them compendiously stated in
didactic form, one may read the French *Book of the
Order of Chivalry*,* of which Caxton issued a translation about a year before the *Morte d'Arthur*, "at
the request of a gentle and noble squire." "Which
book," says the printer, "is not requisite for every
common man to have, but to noble gentlemen that

by their virtue intend to come and enter into the
noble order of chivalry, the which in these late days
hath been used according to this book heretofore
written, but forgotten, and the exercises of chivalry
not used, honoured, nor exercised as it hath been in
ancient time." One cannot but be stirred by this, the
translator's, earnest appeal: "O ye knights of England, where is the custom and usage of noble chivalry that was used in those days [of King Arthur]?
What do ye now but go to the baynes [baths], and
play at dice? And some not well advised, use not
honest and good rule, against all order of knighthood.
Leave this, leave it! and read the noble volumes of
Saint Graal, of Launcelot, of Galahad, of Tristram,
of Perseforest,* of Perceval, of Gawain, and many
more. There shall ye see manhood, courtesy and gentleness. And look in latter days of the noble acts
since the Conquest, in King Richard's days Cœur de
Lyon, Edward the first and the third and his noble
sons; Sir Walter Manny; read Froissart; and also behold that victorious and noble King Harry the fifth,
and the captains under him, his noble brethren, the
Earls of Salisbury, Montagu, and many others whose
names shine gloriously by their virtuous noblesse and
acts that they did in the honour of the order of
chivalry. Alas! what do ye but sleep and take ease,
and are all disordered from chivalry?"

If knights in the fifteenth century were unfaith-

ful to the avowed principles of their order, who then
kept these principles alive? Where was the sanctuary
of that greatest of chivalric virtues, Truth? A short
poem of the time explains:

> *A man that should of Truth tell,*
> *With great lords he may not dwell.*
> *In true story, as clerks tell,*
> *Truth is put in low degree.*
> *In ladies' chambers cometh he not,*
> *There dare Truth get no foot!*
> *Though he would, he may not*
> *Come among the high meiny.*

"In England," as Sir Walter Scott observed, "it was
fortunately not so much the crown as the commons
who rose on the ruins of feudal chivalry." In England men of low degree have often illustrated chivalric character when great lords have acted like churls.

The reading of Malory shows that if nowadays
English-speaking people, high and low alike, respond
instantly to the call of fair play, this is merely a
part of their chivalric inheritance. Frequently it is
emphasized in the *Morte d'Arthur* that there is "no
worship" in taking an opponent at a disadvantage.
We find Sir Lamorak interrupting an unequal strug-
gle, because, he said, "it was shame, four against
one." "Fie for shame," Sir Breuse is rebuked; "strike
never a knight when he is on the earth." "Though
this knight be never so false," said Pelleas about
Gawain, "I will never slay him sleeping; for I will

never destroy the high order of knighthood." Sir Launcelot, observing a fight, undertook "to help the weaker party [the under dog, as it were] in increasing of his chivalry." But there are deeper truths in the knightly ideal, which Malory and chivalric writers in general also help us to grasp. Sir Balin said: "Worthiness and good qualities and good deeds are not all only in arrayment, but manhood and worship is hid within man's person." "Humility and patience," a hermit explained to Gawain, "those be the things that be always green and quick; for [to the end that] man may no time overcome humility and patience, therefore was the Round Table founded, and chivalry hath been at all times."

IV

ACCORDING to the Old French *Order*, "God and chivalry concord together." In that work, however, nothing is said of the courtly love which is essential in the matter of Britain. Malory shows no special fondness for this courtly love, but he could not write a *Morte d'Arthur* and leave it out. Though he necessarily dwells on the amours of his chief heroines, he betrays no quickening enthusiasm for the theme. It would have been difficult, we must admit, so to humanize the ordinary account of Guinevere's intrigue with Launcelot as to fill anyone with tremors of excitement. Even Chrétien de Troyes in the begin-

ning was unable to make it seem other than artificial, and it lost any real life it ever had when elon-
gated in tedious prose. But the same cannot be said
of the passion of Tristram and Ysolt. We are thrilled
to this hour by the early poems on their unconquer-
able love. If Malory did not give us something
similarly exquisite and moving, it was primarily, of
course, because the works of such men as Thomas
and Béroul were inaccessible to him, yet also, we
can but think, because of his own serious nature
and his moral aim in the composition of his book.

We are indeed informed that "to tell the joy
there was between La Belle Isoud and Sir Tristram,
there is no tongue can tell it, nor heart think it, nor
pen write it;" but Malory made no effort to display
the turbulent emotions of either hero or heroine.
The chief reason, in his opinion, why Tristram deserved praise, appears in the following passage, which
has peculiar interest as exhibiting the training of
young English noblemen in his time. Tristram is
first sent for seven years into France, "to learn the
language and nurture, and deeds of arms." "And
after as he growed in might and strength he laboured
ever in hunting and hawking, so that never gentleman more that ever we heard tell of. And the book
saith, he began good measure of blowing of beasts of
venery, of hawking and hunting. And therefore the
book of venery, of hawking and hunting, is called

the book of Sir Tristram. Wherefore, as me seemeth, all gentlemen who bear old arms ought of right to honour Sir Tristram for the goodly terms that gentlemen have and use, and shall to the day of doom, that thereby in a manner all men of worship may dissever a gentleman from a yeoman, and from a yeoman a villain. For he that is gentle will draw unto him gentle taches [qualities], and follow the customs of noble gentlemen."

"Now," says the author on another occasion, "turn we unto Sir Tristram and La Belle Isoud, how they make great joy daily together with all manner of mirths that they could devise." But without adding more on this theme, over which the brilliant Anglo-Norman Thomas lingered with such satisfaction, he immediately continues: "And every day Sir Tristram would ride a-hunting, for Sir Tristram was that time called the best chaser in the world, and the noblest blower of an horn of all manner of measures. For, as books report, of him came all the good terms of venery and hunting, and all the sizes and measures of blowing of an horn; and of him we had first all the terms of hawking, and which were beasts of chase, and beasts of venery, and which were vermins; and all the blasts that belong to all manner of games; first to the uncoupling, to the seeking, to the rechate, to the flight, to the death, and to strake; and many other blasts and terms, that all manner of gentlemen have cause to the world's end to praise Sir Tristram and to pray for his soul." There can be little question that Malory himself loved hunting and thought it preëminently a gentleman's pursuit. So it has remained in England to our day.*

On Sir Launcelot Malory lavishes more superlatives than on any other knight. He is the biggest and the best breathed, the worshipfullest, the marvellousest, the courtliest, the noblest, the most honoured of high and low—and this "in all the world." He is the flower of knights, a man of might matchless, peerless of courtesy. Yet, notwithstanding, he also appears in the *Morte d'Arthur*, as in every romance where he is represented as the father of Galahad, and made to participate in the Quest of the Holy Grail, in the rôle of a sad and sorry sinner, because he "trusted more in his harness than in his Maker," but above all because he had done all his great deeds less in honour of God than in adoration of Guinevere. "For, as the book saith, had not Sir Launcelot been in his privy thoughts and in his mind so set inwardly to the queen, as he was in seeming outward to God, there had been no knights passed him in the quest of the Sangreal."

When one reviews the relations of Launcelot and Guinevere, as presented by Malory, it is plain that Launcelot reveals himself in word and deed as much

the nobler of the two. Guinevere is altogether lacking in humility, patience, or other Christian virtue.
When she heard of her lover's conduct with Elaine,
"she writhed and weltered as a mad woman." When
she saw him bear in a tourney the sleeve of the Maid
of Astolat, "she was well nigh out of her mind for
wrath." On this occasion, she at first refused to see
Launcelot or to let him explain; then finally, when
the facts of his great loyalty were revealed, she still
rebuked him, but now for too little "bounty and gentleness" to her rival—who is dead! "This is not the
first time," said Sir Launcelot, "that ye have been
displeased with me causeless; but, madam, ever I
must suffer you, but what sorrow I endure I take no
force." It is Guinevere who, when Launcelot would
spare her captor, Meliagraunce, gives him a sign to
fight to a finish and revenge by death the insult to
her. Launcelot is impelled to take every sort of risk
for her sake. He recks not for himself; but he is loth
to see her dishonoured. His chivalry is in reality only
personal idealism, which benefits him morally more
than it does the lady he serves.

Launcelot loved but one, and that, according to
Malory, by reason of right. "For to take my pleasure with paramours," the hero declares, "that will I
refuse, in principal for dread of God, for knights that
be adulterous or wanton shall not be happy or fortunate, and who that so useth shall be unhappy and all

thing is unhappy that is about them." Yet, despite
its perfect fidelity, Malory presents his paragon's love
for Guinevere as a grievous offence. It superinduced
the great catastrophe of the fall of the Round Table
fellowship and the death of the king. After her
"most noble lord" departed this life, Guinevere re-
tired to Amesbury, "and there she let make herself
a nun . . . and great penance she took, as ever did sinful lady in this land." She finally renounced Launcelot's love, which he came again to proffer her there,
lest she should endanger her "soul's health," trusting
after her death "to have a sight of the blessed face
of Christ, . . . for as sinful as ever I was are saints
in Heaven." These are her last words to her lover:
"Therefore, Sir Launcelot, go to thy realm, and there
take thee a wife, and live with her with joy and bliss,
and I pray thee heartily, pray for me to Our Lord,
that I may amend my mis-living." But, as she "took
herself to perfection," so thereupon did Launcelot
too; the rest of his days he lived in penance and
hardship, attaining through deep contrition to such
great holiness that at last "the gates of Heaven
opened against him."

Dante seems to have been as much impressed as
Malory by Launcelot's pious manner of ending his
days. Long before, in the *Convivio*, he thus moralized
the tale: " O, wretched and vile, who with hoisted sails
rush into this port [of natural death], and where ye

ought to rest shatter yourselves in the full strength
of the wind and lose yourselves in the very place to
which ye have made so long a voyage. Verily the
knight Launcelot would not enter there with hoisted
sails; nor our most noble Latin Guido of Monte-
feltro. In truth, these noble ones lowered the sails
of the activities of the world; for in their advanced
age they gave themselves to religious orders, putting aside every mundane delight and activity."

Malory expresses his personal feeling frankly and
finely in the following words: "For like as winter
rasure doth always arase and deface green summer,
so fareth it by *unstable love* in man and woman. For
in many persons there is no stability, for we may
see all day, for a little blast of winter's rasure, anon
we shall deface and lay apart *true love* for little or
naught, that cost much thing. This is no wisdom nor
stability, but it is feebleness of nature and great
disworship whosoever useth this. Therefore, like as
May month flowereth and flourisheth in many gar-
dens, so in likewise let every man of worship flourish
his heart in this world, first unto God and next unto
the joy of them he promised his faith unto, for there
never was worshipful man nor worshipful woman,
but they loved one better than another: and worship
in arms may never be foiled, but first reserve the
honour to God, and secondly the quarrel must come
of thy lady: and such call I *virtuous love*. But now-

adays men cannot love seven night but they must
have all their desires, that love may not endure by
reason; for where they be soon accorded, and hasty
heat, soon it cooleth. Right so fareth *love nowadays;* soon hot, soon cold. This is no stability, but
the *old love* was not so. Men and women could love
together seven years, and no wanton lusts were between them, and *then was love truth and faithfulness.*
And lo, in like wise was used *love in King Arthur's
days."**

Guinevere was captious and unreasonable to her
lover, as well as unfaithful to her husband; Morgain
la Fée afflicted Ascolon by her "false lusts;" Vivien
deceived Merlin, who was "assotted" upon her; and
Ettard brought on herself the scorn of all ladies and
gentlewomen because of the pride she manifested
towards King Pelleas, who "chose her for his sovereign lady, and never to love other but her." But, on
the other hand, there are many beautiful ladies in the
Morte d'Arthur who seem the incarnation of gentleness, devotion, and truth. Balin bitterly laments that
he interfered with the true love of Lanceor and his
lady Colombe: by accident he slew "two hearts in
one body," for the lady "slew herself with her lover's
sword for dole and sorrow" at his death. "I have
given," avows Elaine, " the greatest riches and fairest flower that ever I had, and that is my maiden love
and faith." She desired Launcelot's presence "liefer

than all the gold that is above the earth;" she died of her "fervent love." "Now blessed be God, said the fair Maid of Astolat, that that knight sped so well, for he is the man in the world that I first loved, and truly he shall be the last that ever I shall love."

Throughout Malory's book, true love is exalted as a noble inspiration to valour. "Well I wot that love is a great mistress," spoke his chief hero concerning the fate of Palamides, a mighty warrior, who loved Isolt long and faithfully without guerdon. "She hath been the cause of my worship," declared Palamides, "and else I had been the most simplest knight in the world. For by her and because of her, I have won the worship that I have." "I proffered her no dishonour ... I offended never as to her person." "I shall love her to the uttermost days of my life."

"Madam, said Sir Launcelot[to the Queen], I love not to be constrained to love; for love must arise of the heart and not by no constraint. That is truth, said the king, and many knights: love is free in himself, and never will be bounden; for when he is bounden he loseth himself." These words carry us back to the memorable passage in Chaucer's Franklin's Tale, with which they are fully in accord:

> *Love wol nat ben constreyned by maistrye;*
> *Whan maistrie cometh, the god of love anon*
> *Beteth his winges, and farewel! he is gon!*
> *Love is a thing as any spirit free.*

They carry us forward also to Spenser's transformation of Chaucer's lines:

All loss is less and less the infamy,
Than loss of love to him that loves but one:
Ne may love be compelled by mastery:
For soon as mastery comes sweet love anon
Taketh his nimble wings and soon away is gone.

No English poet, however, has exhibited chivalric love, based on truth and faithfulness, more charmingly than Malory's unknown contemporary, the author of the *Nut Brown Maid*.

Though it be sung
Of old and young
  That I should be to blame,
Theirs be the charge
That speak so large
  In hurting of my name:
For I will prove
That faithful love
  It is devoid of shame.

In your distress
And heaviness
  To part with you the same,
To show all to
That do not so
  True lovers are they none;
For in my mind,
Of all mankind,
  I love but you alone.

In an epoch when such a lyric as the *Nut Brown*

Maid could be composed, neither true poetry nor true love was dead.

Sidney, who praised Edward IV above all kings of England,

> *only for this worthy knight durst prove*
> *To lose his crown rather than fail his love,*

and who attributed his own success in "martial sports" to his adored lady—

> *Stella looked on, and from her heavenly face*
> *Sent forth the beams which made so fair my race—*

was later to write of purity in love:

> *If that be sin which doth the manners frame,*
> *Well stayed with truth in word, and faith of deed,*
> *Ready of wit and fearing naught but shame;*
> *If that be sin which in fixed hearts doth breed*
> *A loathing of all loose unchastity:*
> *Then love is sin, and let me sinful be.*

Finally, in this connection, it deserves note that almost the only instance of happy *wedded* love in the entire *Morte d'Arthur* is that of the wife of King Meliodas, the mother of Sir Tristram; she was "a full meek lady and well she loved her lord, and he her again, and the time came that she should bear a child, so there was great joy betwixt them." Malory, we may well believe, favoured wedded love as much as Chaucer, but his material gave him little chance to make that clear.

V

Chaucer spoke of the Book of Launcelot as one
that "women hold in full great reverence;" he knew
Launcelot as a pattern of courtliness; but there was
another Arthurian hero for whom he had greater
enthusiasm—"Gawayne with his olde curteisye."
Anyone who knows Gawain only from the *Morte
d'Arthur* has contempt for him, since (with some exceptions, relics of the older presentation) he is there
pictured as envious, revengeful, merciless, a troth-
breaker, and light of love. Never was so great cal-
umny put upon a noble warrior. We can understand
it in Malory; but it seems nearly inexcusable that
Tennyson also should have vilified Gawain's name;
and certainly this will be more and more counted
against him as a matter of serious reproach.

There exists in old English a considerable cycle of
poems in which Gawain is exalted, and always con-
sistently, as a knight of peculiar charm and nobility.
Of these we can here examine but one—*Gawain
and the Green Knight.** The unknown fourteenth-
century author of this delightful work displays narrative art of rare excellence. Gaston Paris called the
poem a jewel in our literature; but perhaps it will
always be best understood by Englishmen, so subtly
does it gratify their taste. The poet shows keen sen-
sitiveness to nature in all its English moods, the
dreary as well as the glad; he describes English land-

scapes of different sorts with striking vividness; his festival and hunting scenes are surrounded with the national atmosphere of mirth. Above all, we sympathize with his conception of the hero's character: Gawain is here pictured as strong and vigorous, ready to travel solitary paths without fear or wavering, gracious in speech and courteous in manner, loyal in allegiance and sensitive to honour, beloved of all and envied of none. In contrast with him, Launcelot is too conventional, too artificial, too *mondain* for robust Englishmen, who have always preferred an outdoor to a social knight. It is noteworthy that Malory makes Gawain—as Shakespeare makes Hotspur—suspicious of a smooth talker. "Make thou no more language, said Sir Gawain [to Sir Launcelot], but deliver the queen from thee, and pike thee lightly out of this court." "Then Sir Gawain said: 'Sir Launcelot, and thou darest do battle, leave thy babbling and come off, and let us ease our hearts.'" It is Gawain who arouses Arthur to say to his enemy: "Fie upon thy fair language."

In the fifteenth century, the English had also heroes of the forests in whom they took delight, ballad-heroes, like Robin Hood. We cannot be too grateful that the ballads of Robin Hood were conceived in the age of chivalry, for in them Robin seems almost as courteous and loveable as Gawain himself. Shakespeare thought of the noble outlaw when de-

scribing the care-free life of the gentle duke, father
of Rosalind.

> *In summer, when the shaws be sheen,*
> *And leaves be large and long:*
> *It is full merry in fair forest*
> *To hear the foulës song:*
>
> *To see the deer draw to the dale,*
> *And leave the hillës hee*
> *And shadow 'em in the leavës green,*
> *Under the greenwood tree.*

With what joy we repeat these words! They themselves are "full merry." The author of *Gawain and
the Green Knight* describes a scene at merry Christ-
mas in merry England. The word "merry" is likewise ever on Malory's lips. It is English to the core.
"Gay" to us savours of the *salon;* "merry" has the
perfume of new-mown hay in the fields—the fair
fields of a happy land. In England it is believed that
God made the country, and man made the town. To
the French France is *douce* or *belle*, but to us England
is "old" or "merry;" and long vistas of national difference disclose themselves in these characteristic
adjectives of praise.

Like a true Englishman, Malory loved "the merry
month of May." In a charming little chapter, in
which he likens true love to summer, he sings a paean
to "that lusty month," which "giveth unto all lovers
courage;" "for like as herbs and trees bring forth

fruit and flourish in May, in likewise every lusty heart, that is in any manner a lover, springeth and flourisheth in lusty deeds. . . . For then all herbs and trees renew a man and woman, and in likewise lovers call again to their mind old gentleness and old service, and many kind deeds that were forgotten by negligence."

Numerous English stories of old gentleness and old service have been forgotten by negligence, on our own part or that of our ancestors. Some of great interest have been preserved by Malory alone. One of these relates how, at a high feast of Pentecost in Carlisle, Sir Launcelot healed the wounds of Sir Urry, a knight of Hungary, which had been inflicted by enchantment. He was unwilling to try the cure after all his fellows had failed, for fear of the appearance of presumption. But his sovereign insisted, and, when Launcelot had success, "then King Arthur and all the kings and knights knelt down, and gave thanks and lovings unto God and to His blessed mother, and ever Sir Launcelot wept as a child that had been beaten." In this scene Launcelot has probably usurped the place of another hero, but whoever acted as he did is a knight unto whom, in Malory's phrase, "our hearts give greatly." He had the meekness of true chivalry.

The most original part of the *Morte d'Arthur*, however, is that which sets forth the *enfances* of Sir

Gareth, of whom mention has already been made. It is improbable that this story ever passed through the hydraulic press of late French prose, for it is not sapped of delightful freshness. Malory's words are here specially full of vigour, and his phrases more tinged with homely realism than anywhere else. We gladly applaud young Gareth, because, while bewilderingly successful in arms, he is ever modest, and because, though "he had great labour for his love," he yet so persevered, with astonishing self-restraint, that his love's labour was not lost. "I would fain be of good fame and knighthood," he says; and he conquers every obstacle set in his path—moral obstacles of unfair scorn and undeserved recrimination, as well as the physical impediments of dreary ways, and opponents without mercy and pity. For the sake of his honour and Arthur's, he engages in a fierce succession of fights, and then in a great tournament "paineth himself and enforceth himself to do great deeds" so as to show himself best beloved with his lady. "This Sir Gareth was a noble knight and a well ruled and a fair languaged"—so ends the story of his brilliant career. Certainly, not only by reputation, but also by his conduct in instances recorded, he appears in Malory's book as Launcelot describes him in maturity—"a gentle knight, courteous, true and bounteous, meek and mild, and in him is no manner of mal-engine, but plain, faithful and true."

The words "meek and mild" applied here to
Gareth, as elsewhere to Launcelot, remind us of the
persistent union of the phraseology as well as the
principles of chivalry and religion. One of the most
favoured hymns now sung in English churches opens
with the words "Gentle Jesu, meek and mild."
There is evidently something of mysticism in Malory's book. Often while reading it, we seem to be
within a solemn Gothic cathedral, where processions
pass and organ notes resound; incense rises and
chants die away; but a great sense of mystery remains. In an atmosphere remote from that of the
world, unreal for the body, the soul seems to be
lifted up, to perceive the higher verities of life. "By
the Round Table," Malory tells us, " is the whole
world signified by right."

VI

THE question of lineage as allied to gentleness continued in the reactionary age after Chaucer to occupy the public thought. " It is contrary to the laws
of nature," said the Scot Henryson, "for a gentleman to be degenerate, not following of his primo-
geniture the worthy rule."

> *The nobleness and great magnificence*
> *Of prince or lord, who lists to magnify,*
> *His great ancestry and lineal descents*
> *Should first extol, and his genealogy,*
> *So that his heart he might incline thereby*

The more to virtue and to worthiness,
*Hearing rehearse his elders' gentleness.**

In the fifteenth century the difference between *no-biles* and *ignobiles*, between gentlemen and others, was made more manifest than before by the privilege, strictly denied all but the former, to use coat-armour. In 1415, when Henry V was preparing for his French campaign, he issued a proclamation that no man should bear arms without proving by what ancestral right or by whose gift he bore them, and claims were to be submitted to officers appointed for the purpose. Infringements on the rights of gentlemen, or disputes that concerned them as such—disputes of honour—were dealt with by the so-called Court of Chivalry. This court was a very powerful body in Malory's time. By its authority, a knight might be "degraded" for unbecoming conduct, and his coat-of-arms reversed, after which he was considered as dead in chivalry; or he might have blots put on his 'scutcheon—"abatements," they were called —for all sorts of "ungentle" acts.

Malory nowhere gives a hint that there might be any sort of gentleman in the land but one of station. To him the gentleman is exactly the French *gentilhomme*. The commons, or commonalty, are mentioned only a few times in his book, and never with consideration. That he did not leave them out simply because they had little to do with knightly story is evident from the fact that he included certain incidents and reflections, which he might have omitted if he had desired, but with the tone of which he seems, on the contrary, to have been in full sympathy.

After telling, for example, of the way that the noble knight Hermance, noted for "his goodness and gentleness," was deceived and slain by two false knights, not of his own blood, to whom he had entrusted his affairs, Malory writes: "It is an old saw, Give a churl rule, and thereby he will not be sufficed; for whatsoever he be that is ruled by a villain born, and the lord of the soil to be a gentleman born, the same villain shall destroy all the gentlemen about him; therefore all estates and lords beware whom ye take about you."

One day, on the occasion of the king's marriage, Aries, a cowherd, brings to Arthur a youth, Tor, whom he supposes to be his own son, and asks that he be knighted. Tor, he declares, is very unlike him and his other sons in interests and qualities, and the boy shows this difference in visage and behaviour. All marvel how it could be that a cowherd's son had gentle traits. Merlin must needs explain that he is really the son of King Pellinore, begotten by that stern knight on the "fair house-wife" before her marriage to Aries, "when she was a maid and went to milk kine." Sir Tor succeeds in his first quest of arms, and Pellinore then proposes him for admission to the Round Table. Arthur observes with gratification that "he saith little, and he doth much more," and agrees to receive him; but he does not withhold this significant remark: "I know none in all this court, *and he were as well born on his mother's side as he is on your side,* that is like him of prowess and might."

Sir Gareth also came to Arthur's court an unknown young man, and at first asked Arthur for nothing but to give him meat and drink for a twelvemonth. "My fair son," said Arthur, "ask better, I counsel thee, for this is but a simple asking, for my heart giveth me to thee greatly that thou art come of men of worship." Arthur could evidently tell a gentleman when he saw him; but Kay, the crabbed steward, into whose charge the youth was given, believed him a "villain born" and set him menial tasks. "And so he endured all that twelvemonth and never displeased man nor child, but always he was meek and mild." Soon afterwards he started on a mission, to succour a lady in distress, accompanied by a damsel-messenger, who reproached him all the way for his low birth; but Gareth acted towards her with such unfailing courtesy that finally she was constrained to say: "O mercy, marvel have I, . . . what manner of man ye be, for it may never be otherwise but that ye be come of a noble blood, for so foully and shamefully did never woman rule

a knight as I have done you, and ever courteously
ye have suffered me, and that came never but of
gentle blood."

In the *Book of St. Albans* (printed in 1486, a year
after the *Morte d'Arthur*) we read that "all gentleness comes of God of Heaven," and we at first think
that this is exactly the sentiment of Chaucer: "Gentilesse cometh from God alone;" but we are soon un-
deceived: the St. Albans writer is merely endeavour-
ing to show that heraldry began above. Admitting
that "all were created in Heaven in gentle nature,"
he emphasizes the fact that Lucifer "with millions
out of Heaven fell into hell and other places and
be holden there in bondage." Then, having in mind
Wat Tyler's cry, he remarks: "A bondman or a churl
will say all we be come of Adam. So Lucifer with
his company may say all we be come of Heaven"—
surely a sufficient retort!

Naïvely, or perhaps subtly, the writer continues:
"Now for to divide gentlemen from churls, in haste
it shall be proved. There was never gentleman nor
churl ordained by kind but he had father and mother.
Adam and Eve had neither father nor mother, and
in the sons of Adam and Eve was found both gentleman and churl. By the sons of Adam and Eve,
Seth, Abel, and Cain, divided was the royal blood
from the ungentle. A brother to slay his brother
contrary to the law, where might be more ungen-

tleness? By that did Cain become a churl and all his
offspring after him, by the cursing of God and his
own father Adam. And Seth was made a gentleman
through his father's and mother's blessing. And of
the offspring of Seth Noah came, a gentleman by
kind. Noah had three sons begotten by kind. By the
mother two were named Ham and Shem, and by
the father the third was named Japhet. Yet in these
three sons gentleness and ungentleness was found.
In Ham ungentleness was found to his own father
done to discover his privities and laugh his father
to scorn. Japhet was the youngest and reproved his
brother. Then let a gentleman take mind of Ham,
for ungentleness he was become a churl and had
the cursing of God and his father Noah." "Of the
offspring of the gentleman Japhet came Abraham,
Moses, Aaron, and the prophets, and also the kings
of the right line of Mary, of whom that gentleman
Jesus was born, very God and very man: after his
manhood King of the land of Judea and of Jews,
gentleman by his mother Mary, Prince of cotear-
mure."*

Similar ingenious ideas affected some versions of
the legend of the Holy Grail, and concerning Galahad, a descendant of the "gentle knight," Joseph of
Arimathea, we read in the *Morte d'Arthur:* "He is
of all parties come of the best knights in the world,
and of the highest lineage; for Sir Launcelot is come

but of the eighth degree from our Lord Jesu Christ;
and Sir Galahad is from the ninth degree from our
Lord Jesu Christ; therefore I dare say they be the
greatest gentlemen of the world." This pedigree is as
absurd as possible; but no one will deny that it implies the highest sort of obligation for a man of rank.

"Now, fair Sir, said Galahad [to the son of a King
of Denmark], since ye be come of kings and queens,
now look that knighthood be well set in you, for
ye *ought* to be a mirror unto all chivalry." Chaucer
writes: "He is gentle who doth gentle deeds." Malory insists: "He who is gentle ought to do gentle
deeds"—*Noblesse oblige.*

Malory believed in the established order of things,
the ascendency of the nobles, but not as one indif-
ferent to corruption or injustice. He would have had
the lords of his day reform themselves, and he would
have conducted the reform on the basis of idealistic principle, — the pressure to change coming from
within, spiritual, rather than from without, temporal.
He would not have wished to overthrow the consti-
tution of knighthood when it no longer perfectly fulfilled the object of its being: he would have amended
it so that it might still prevail for good. Malory was
serious, earnest, high-souled. He loved his country,
"the noble realm of England," and though inflexible
in class feeling, he was undoubtedly a force for right-

eousness in his day. Because of just such men as he, the English aristocracy has long been honoured, nay beloved.

In England there has never been so definite a cleavage between the different ranks of society as exists on the Continent. In England noble birth seldom ensures a title to others than the eldest born of a family, and there are at present innumerable gentlemen in the realm of better lineage than many of the peers. This fact has been an endless aid to the maintenance of knightly ideals among the people at large. Chivalry has not concerned the titled alone. Commoners and aristocrats alike have striven to exhibit the noble qualities which Malory led them to admire in the heroes of the Round Table. Through the *Morte d'Arthur* the whole nation has come better to comprehend the virtue of chivalry—its beauty and its holiness.

SPENSER

SPENSER

THE era of Edward III and Poictiers is gone; the era of Henry V and Agincourt is gone; come have "the spacious times of great Elizabeth" and the Armada of Spain. Wat Tyler's social revolt is past; Jack Cade's political rebellion is past; cultivated men now strive for Protestantism and educational reform. Legends and *fabliaux* are out of date; romances and *chansons de geste*, even in prose, are out of date; in vogue are sonnets, pastorals, and intellectual conceits; the mighty drama has just begun to stretch its giant limbs. Chaucer and Spenser are roughly two hundred years apart. We have left the Middle Ages and are in the full flush of the English Renaissance.

However we may regard Spenser to-day, it is evident that he was a godsend to English letters in the sixteenth century. No one could question his learning, his refinement, his dignity. He was in sympathy with humanism; he was at ease in polite circles; he emulated the noblest masters of poetic art. Still more, natural genius distinguished him "like a pearl among white peas." He was fresh and original while most of his fellows merely retained impressions, or reproduced borrowed thoughts. His astonishing mastery of rhyme, his mellifluousness of phrase, and his rich fecundity of imagination made him rank first among the writers of his time. Where Spenser led, English poetry was likely to go. Had he been disdainful of the literary past of his nation, he might have hindered that precious continuity so remarkable in English verse. Fortunately Spenser felt the conscience of Englishmen in accord with his own, and he did much to establish their purest conceptions of morality, and their highest hopes for the public weal. He attached himself reverentially to English traditions in letters, cementing the old with the new in firm, permanent bonds. Perhaps the very dreaminess of his great allegory made it the more potent in perpetuating love of chivalrous deeds. Systematic arguments would never have overcome the harsh judgements of mediaeval life which men had proudly begun to pass. The *Faery Queen* was, as it were, a soft answer turning away the wrath of reformers. All yielded to its charm, and knighthood was again sheltered from neglect.

Times without number since the day of Lamb, Spenser has been called the poets' poet. This name, however, we must repeat again, because it indicates the chief means of his influence in fixing chivalric ideals in English hearts. Whoever reads any significant amount of modern English verse is sure to imbibe some of Spenser's spirit, since that our best poets still love to cherish and maintain.

> *For deeds do die, however nobly done,*
> *And thoughts of men do as themselves decay;*
> *But wise words, taught in numbers for to run,*
> *Recorded by the Muses, live for aye.*

I

"I NEVER look upon an author," said Montaigne, "be he such as write of virtue and of actions, but I curiously endeavour to find out what he was himself." There are certain aspects of Spenser's career which, for the better understanding of his attitude, it is important to note.

He spent his boyhood in London—"merry London," he calls it, "my most kindly nurse." London in the second half of the sixteenth century was a refreshing, stimulating place in which to live, a city not yet given over to Puritanism and business, to the sombre and the dull. Elizabeth, "the fairest princess under sky," dwelt in this "fair Cleopolis," and was surrounded by admirers who believed with the poet himself:

> *Well beseems all knights of noble name*
> *That covet in th' immortal book of fame*
> *To be eterniz'd, that same to haunt,*
> *And do their service to that sovereign dame,*
> *That glory does to them for guerdon grant:*
> *For she is heavenly born, and heaven may justly vaunt.*

Spenser early felt the claim of social gaiety and courtliness; he saw them everywhere in public in his youth. He also early learned what it meant for a nation to be grave; he was born in the very year that Bloody Mary ascended the throne; he was nineteen when the dreadful massacre of St. Bartholomew occurred.

Though his immediate family was obscure, Spenser prided himself that he came of "an house of ancient fame," and this incited him to seek personal renown. Though technically a gentleman, he was nevertheless sufficiently apart from men of station to make him brood upon his rank and be anxious for the consideration of those more favoured in the world's eyes. "The nobility of the Spensers," declared Gibbon, "has been illustrated and enriched by the trophies of Marlborough; but I exhort them to consider the *Faery Queen* as the most precious jewel of their coronet." No statement by one competent to judge would have given the author of that work more definite delight.

Passing from the Merchant Taylors' School (then newly founded), he went, at about the age of seventeen, to Cambridge, and entered Pembroke Hall. Cambridge was his "mother," but he does not say "benign." There, in any case, he found "many a gentle muse and many a learned wit." There he began to read and love the ancient poets and philosophers, Plato above all. His chief friends were Gabriel Harvey (already a fellow of his college) and a comrade undergraduate, Edward Kirke. The former was a man of dominating personality, but self-satisfied, pedantic, and vain, preaching in season and out of season the humanities, yet with little sympathy for any opinions save his own. He disdained earlier Eng-

lish verse, tried to get Spenser to imitate Latin me-
tres, and sniffed at his plan for the *Faery Queen*. Had
he had his way, our poet would have been dwarfed.

Edward Kirke, a much more amiable person,
whose appreciation of his friend was very high, later
became his introducer to the public, writing a flatter-
ing introduction and copious glosses to Spenser's first
important poem, the *Shepherd's Calendar*, evidently
with the author's help and approval. This introduction took the form of a letter to Harvey, and contains an interesting, though not altogether convincing, defence of "the new poet's" use of archaic words.
It begins with a quotation from "the old famous poet
Chaucer," who is frequently alluded to in the work
as Tityrus, being thus compared to Virgil, and for
whom both he and the author show genuine esteem.
Kirke also quotes Lydgate, "a worthy scholar of so
excellent a master," and refers to Skelton. Spenser
himself alludes to Langland in "the Pilgrim that the
Ploughman played a while," so that previous English
writers were evidently not neglected by this brilliant
group of Cambridge clerks. Still, their chief thoughts
seem elsewhere. The *Shepherd's Calendar* was a series of eclogues—an ambitious experiment, to test,
we are told, the poet's ability—and his models were
foreigners old and new. "So flew Virgil, so flew Man-
tuan . . . so Petrarch . . . so Boccace . . . so Marot,
Sanazarus, and also divers other excellent both Ital-

ian and French poets, whose footing this author everywhere followeth; yet so as few, but they be well-scented, can trace him out."

The *Shepherd's Calendar* was dedicated to Sir Philip Sidney, "president of noblesse and of chivalry," and with this famous hero Spenser had the good fortune to reside for a while at Penshurst. Sidney presented him to his uncle, the Earl of Leicester, who also invited the poet to visit him at his house in London, in the Strand. In his *Prothalamion*, Spenser refers to the "gifts and goodly grace" which he received from this great lord; and praises also his friend, the Earl of Essex, "fair branch of honour, flower of chivalry," for his prowess and victorious arms. While still open to impression, Spenser came into intimate relationship with some of the most distinguished noblemen of the period, who were either writers themselves or patrons of letters. They saw the greatest era of English literature dawn in majesty.

The effect that association with Sir Philip Sidney and his group had upon Spenser, especially in his view of chivalry, we have every reason to believe great. Though Sidney died at thirty-one, his is yet a name to conjure with for all who admire virtuous strength. No Englishman has ever impressed his own or later times as a more perfect type of gentleman, "in whom the life itself of true worth did (by way of example) far exceed the pictures of it by any moral precepts." "The truth is," wrote Fulke Greville, Lord Brooke, "his end was not writing, nor his knowledge moulded for tables nor schools; but both his art and his understanding bent upon his heart to make himself and others, not in words or opinion, but in life and action, good and great." "This was it which, I profess, I loved dearly in him, and still shall be glad to honour in the great men of this time: I mean that his heart and tongue went both one way, *and so with everyone that went with the truth,* knowing no other kindred, party, or end."

All are familiar with the story of the greatness of heart that Sidney showed when wounded at Zutphen. His words when he gave the poor soldier the water he was himself about to drink, "thy necessity is yet greater than mine," have echoed down the centuries. Similarly, Englishmen remember, with applause, Sidney's attitude in death. "The last scene in this tragedy," says his biographer, "was the parting between the two brothers, the weaker showing infinite strength in suppressing sorrow, and the stronger infinite weakness in expressing it." As Malory said of Arthur, "he was so full of knighthood that knightly he endured the pain."

What the Earl of Warwick was to Malory, and probably much more, Sir Philip Sidney was to Spenser—a visible embodiment of superlatively high knightly conduct, "a sea-mark raised upon [his] native coast" by which he as well as the whole nation might "learn to sail, through the straits of true virtue, into a calm and spacious ocean of humane honour." Matthew Roydon found in him

> *A sweet attractive kind of grace,*
> *A full assurance given by looks,*
> *Continual comfort in a face,*
> *The lineaments of gospel books.*

In this worthy man, this man of virtuous name, love and honour did agree. Like the brave Chevalier Bayard, almost a contemporary, he lived *sans peur et sans reproche.*

Spenser was in Ireland when Sidney died, and there he wrote an elegy in his friend's praise, bewailing his own grievous loss. The greater part of Spenser's time of poetic composition he lived in Ireland. He went there first as secretary to the "most renowned and valiant" governor, Lord Grey of Wilton, to whom he acknowledged himself "bound by vassalage," and remained after the latter's departure, in one or another minor official position, with sufficient income for his needs, plenty of opportunity to refresh himself physically and imaginatively amid beautiful scenes, plenty of time to study and write. But Spenser felt himself an exile, and longed for London. Possessed of a querulous nature, he encouraged discontent by brooding over his remoteness from any large centre of civilization. He had begun his *Faery Queen* before he went abroad. His instinct had led him to romance, and allegory complied with the bent he received from collegiate cultivation. Probably, however, both aspects of his work were strengthened by his solitary residence in a land he found savage and wild, where his life seemed like knight-errantry of old. He was led in isolation to dream dreams of book-worthies and to view facts at home in unreal semblance.

The most sympathetic person whom Spenser saw in his frontier abode was "the right noble and valorous Sir Walter Raleigh, Knight," to whom he was eventually to expound the intention of the *Faery Queen* in an open letter prefixed to the first edition of that work. Spenser describes Raleigh as his "sovereign goddess's most dear delight," and indeed he was greatly indebted to Raleigh, as he himself declares, for "singular favours and sundry good turns" shown to him when later he visited England, especially his presentation to the queen. It was Raleigh who had persuaded him to revisit London and take his poem there for publication, and his influence helped Spenser greatly ("neither envying other nor envied") in putting him into relations with the great of the metropolis, in association with whom he was ever soothed and caressed. Spenser termed Raleigh "Shepherd of the Ocean," and he must always have been quickened by the conversation of this intrepid traveller, gentle courtier, and highly gifted man of letters.

In early days, just after leaving college, the poet had become enamoured of a lady in Lancashire whom he calls Rosalind, and had taken her as the inspiration of his verse, though we cannot believe that she was a much more real personage, as he describes her, than many another object of sonnet love. But while there is also a good deal that is purely imaginative in the account of his love for the fair Irish lady, Elizabeth Boyle, whom, after years of wooing, he finally won, his affection for her appears profound, and called forth his most exquisite lyric, his marvellously delicate and finely-perfected *Epithalamium*.

Twice, during his residence in Ireland, Spenser returned home, each time with a garner of poesy to present the world, and each time he heard renewed the compliments that had greeted him as author of the *Shepherd's Calendar*. Yet he grew increasingly forlorn. He felt that poets were not held in deserved honour, that parasites and sycophants had too great share of official reward. Vain expectations and idle hopes, he himself states, affected his brain. It is to be feared that Spenser was not easy to satisfy, and that he was himself partly to blame for his lack of delight. He was sorely afflicted by "the scholar's melancholy, which is emulation."

Spenser's career was doomed to a tragic end. By his defiant acts and general unsympathetic attitude, he had angered his Irish neighbours. Finally, they burst upon and burned his Kilcolman house, so that he and his family had to flee for their lives. This deed of terrible violence caused his death; in three months the poet passed away poor and wretched, though his loss was a national grief. With fellow poets following him to the grave, he was laid beside his beloved Chaucer in Westminster Abbey, and over him was written:

> *Here nigh to Chaucer Spenser lies: to whom*
> *In genius next he was, as now in tomb.*

It was, it seems, by Spenser's own request that his bones were given a resting-place beside those of his master —

> *Dan Chaucer, well of English undefiled,*
> *On Fame's eternal beadroll worthy to be filed.*

Spenser's praise for "that renowned poet" is always without stint; but in the following stanza he exalts him most openly and finely as unique among his loves:

> *Then pardon, O most sacred happy spirit!*
> *That I thy labours lost may thus revive,*
> *And steal from thee the meed of thy due merit,*
> *That none durst ever whilst thou wast alive,*
> *And, being dead, in vain yet many strive:*
> *Ne dare I like; but, through infusion sweet*
> *Of thine own spirit, which doth in me survive,*

I follow here the footing of thy feet,
That with thy meaning so I may the rather meet.

Chaucer and Spenser had similar careers. Both
were Londoners of comparatively humble origin,
who, having to make their own way in the world,
early sought the society of the great. Their talents
commended them; they won favour. They were supported by influential patrons and attracted the attention of their respective queens. Both received
royal pensions and official positions. Both participated somewhat in public affairs. But neither lived a
life of tranquil ease, for their offices were no sinecures,
and each suffered the vicissitudes of political dispute.

With so much in common, there is nevertheless
"a long and large difference" between them in other
ways. Chaucer, so far as we know, was not a university man. He picked up his knowledge by the way,
unsystematically, as inclination led and opportunity
offered. Spenser, on the contrary, lived seven years at
Cambridge, and was a careful scholar, well trained in
the classics (including Greek, of which few Englishmen knew a word in his predecessor's days), learned
in philosophy and the poetic art. He was one of an
esoteric group devoted to first-hand studies of the
ancients, working together with lordly zeal for the
improvement of English letters, evincing the radiant
glee, together with the supreme vanity and intem-
perate vexation, of the haughty Renaissance.

In temperament, as well as in intellectual training, the two men were distinctly unlike. They were
both gentle, courteous, refined in manner, sensitive,
and reserved. But Spenser could be harsh in judgement of races, cruelly intolerant of sects, and haugh-
tily disdainful of individuals, which it is impossible
to imagine of friendly Chaucer, whom all loved. Nowhere does Spenser reveal a trace of Chaucer's genial humour. He took himself, his art, everything, in
grave earnest.

Furthermore, while Chaucer willingly lived all the
time in reality, Spenser, it is evident, preferred to
roam musingly in pleasing pastures of fantasy. The
one was best in delineating human beings in open
day, the other in picturing abstractions in "silver
mist." While the *Faery Queen* exhales a rarefied
perfume, which is apt to pall on the robust, Chaucer's verse is eternally fresh, like the spring mornings
when he wandered forth at dawn to hear the birds
sing blissfully and to see the daisies spread against
the sun.

Spenser had a wide mental horizon. He was a
sincere devotee of duty and right. His work is per-
meated with strong patriotism. It is not, however,
the poet's intellectuality or morality or pride of race
that completely commends him to us, but rather his
artistic vitality. His moral seriousness was always
tempered by aesthetic gaiety; he liked to abandon

grave doctrine for frolics of fancy. He tried to make us believe that he sought only virtue, but we feel that he first worshipped at the shrine of beauty. He gave lip-service to learning, but he adored loveliness.

Plainly, Spenser cherished books more than men. He revelled in his well-stored library, sipping the sweet wines of poesy with the joy of the connoisseur. The taste lingered on his palate. He refreshed his emotions. He "lulled his senses in slumber of delight."

> *The ways through which my weary steps I guide*
> *In this delightful land of faery,*
> *Are so exceeding spacious and wide,*
> *And sprinkled with such sweet variety*
> *Of all that pleasant is to ear or eye,*
> *That I,* nigh ravished with rare thoughts delight,
> *My tedious travel do forget thereby.*

So the poet confesses himself. He was, it is clear, a "child of fancy," easy to ridicule, like "magnificent" Armado in *Love's Labour's Lost*, who also strove to tell "in high-born words, the worth of many a knight . . . lost in the world's debate:"

> *A man in all the world's new fashions planted*
> *That hath a mint of phrases in his brain;*
> *One whom the music of his own vain tongue*
> *Doth ravish like enchanting harmony:*
> *A man of complements, whom right and wrong*
> *Have chose as umpire of their mutiny.*

Armado, "plume of feathers," implored his princess in fantastic words to "have commiseration of

[her] heroical vassal!" Similarly, Spenser lauds his
queen in terms of extravagant praise, while pleading for her grace. It is a genuine problem of sincerity
and taste how Spenser could, without any apparent
quiver, turn out upon Elizabeth such cornucopias
of sugared sweets as was his wont. She in her self-
satisfaction might receive them undisturbed, but
what about him? The fact that Spenser accepted for
himself and printed before the *Faery Queen* so many
elaborate encomiums of his friends shows that he did
not balk at much in his own person. He posed, however, as only a simple poet, "Immerito," and she was
"the image of the heavens," "without a mortal blem-
ish," "above all her sex that ever yet had been"!
"The springs both of good and evil," wrote the author
of *Utopia*, "flow from the prince, over a whole nation,
as from a lasting fountain." Elizabeth undoubtedly
contributed much to dignify the English nation, and
one can understand why idealists in times of stress
pictured her as a national Virgin, calling for chivalric loyalty; but to name her "sacred saint" and the
like, as Spenser did, was beyond reason as well as
truth. Spenser's fawnings and flatteries, common
though such were in his day, place both him and his
queen in an unfavourable light. We feel that he was
degraded by pandering to the vanity of Elizabeth,
even as Chaucer was ennobled by association with
Philippa the Good. Chaucer sanely desired to perfect

nature; Spenser strained himself to improve on her in pride.

Spenser has always the mark of distance. As a poet, his imagination "reigned in the air from earth to highest sky;" his "precious odours" were "fetched from far away;" his ideals of beauty, love, and life transcended mortal reach. As a man, likewise, he held himself apart, exclusive, superior, solemnly ambitious to write what should last to eternity. His chief work he strove to make

> *The port of rest from troublous toil,*
> *The world's sweet inn from pain and wearisome turmoil.*

II

An interesting record by one Ludowick Bryskett of a meeting of thoughtful men at his house near Dublin, where Spenser was present, shows that the poet was bountifully esteemed by scholars in Ireland and looked up to as an intellectual guide. It reveals also the serious character of the studies with which he and his associates were then occupied, and throws light on the plan of the *Faery Queen.*

"Herein," said Bryskett to his guests, "do I greatly envy the happiness of the Italians who have in their mother-tongue late writers that have, with a singular easy method, taught all that Plato and Aristotle have confusedly or obscurely left written, of which some I have begun to read with no small delight;

as Alexander·Piccolomini, Gio. Baptista Giraldi, and Guazzo; all three having written upon the ethic part of moral philosophy both exactly and perspicuously. And would God that some of our countrymen would show themselves so well affected to the good of their country (*whereof one principal and most important part consisteth in the instructing men to virtue*), as to set down in English the precepts of those parts of moral philosophy, whereby our youth might, without spending so much time as the learning of those other languages require, speedily enter into the right course of virtuous life."

Thereupon, Bryskett appealed directly to Spenser to help him and his friends by discoursing to them on that theme; entreating him to vouchsafe to open unto them "the goodly cabinet, in which this excellent treasure of virtues is locked up from the vulgar sort." Spenser courteously acknowledged the compliment, but begged to be excused at that time. "I have already undertaken a work," he said, "tending to the same effect, which is in heroical verse under the title of a *Faery Queen*, to represent all the moral virtues, assigning to every virtue a knight to be the patron and defender of the same, in whose actions and feats of arms and chivalry the operations of that virtue, whereof he is the protector, are to be expressed, and the vices and unruly appetites that oppose themselves against the same are to be beaten down and overcome. . . . I have taken in hand to discourse at large in my poem."

If, then, we view the *Faery Queen* as primarily a narrative, we neglect the author's avowed intent. He planned it first and foremost as a book of ethical instruction, with Plato and Aristotle, as well as their disciples and exegetes, definitely in mind. He desired through it to show the operations of virtue and vice, in hope to improve the morals of English youth. Already, in the *Shepherd's Calendar*, he had written:

> *O! what an honour is it to restrain*
> *The lust of lawless youth with good advice,*

and even then he aspired to sing of bloody Mars, of wars, of jousts, letting his muse thereby display her fluttering wing. Spenser did not agree with those who "had rather have good discipline delivered by way of precepts or sermoned at large;" he believed that "much more profitable and gracious is doctrine by ensample than by rule." He was a born poet, "trained in chivalry," albeit "noursled up in lore of learned philosophy." Frankly emulating Homer, Virgil, Ariosto, and Tasso, excellent poets, as he recognized, he wished to portray the image of a brave knight in a work of art. He decided, alas! to present his ideas "cloudily enwrapped in allegorical devices;" he failed to achieve unity of plot; he accomplished but meagrely what he set out to perform; yet only because of its artistic setting has his thought lived.*

"For that I conceived [this] should be most plausible and pleasing, being coloured with an historical fiction, I chose," says the poet, "the history of King Arthur, as most fit for the excellency of his person, being made famous by many men's former works, and also farthest from the danger of envy and suspicion of present time." There can be no question that the glamour which surrounds tales of Arthur and faery has always strengthened the appeal of Spenser's work. The choice of his fiction was wise. Happily, it also tended to confirm his natural inclination to the sentiments of chivalry. Close consideration of mediaeval books of courtesy and romance deepened his devotion to the ideals there glorified. "Unknown, unkissed," he might properly have said to Harvey and his like. Why should he relinquish the tested good of the Middle Ages because he desired also the proffered good of the Renaissance? "How charming is divine philosophy," he felt with his whole heart; but he also exulted in ancient shews of "honour."

> O goodly usage of those antique times
> In which the sword was servant unto right;
> When not for malice and contentious crimes,
> But all for praise, and proof of manly might,
> The martial brood accustomed to fight:
> Then honour was the meed of victory,
> And yet the vanquished had no despight.

The *Faery Queen* is a very paean of chivalry,

whose watchword is honour. "Lo!" the poet exclaims in his opening lines:

> [*I*] *sing of knights and ladies gentle deeds;*
> *Whose praises have slept in silence long.*

Spenser's knights and ladies appear more "thoroughly instructed" than those of Malory, but they engage in the same pursuits:

> *Full many countries they did overrun*
> *From the uprising to the setting sun,*
> *And many hard adventures did achieve;*
> *Of all the which they honour ever won.*
> *Seeking the weak oppressed to relieve*
> *And to recover rights from such as wrong did grieve.*

The "fierce wars and faithful loves" which were to "moralize" the *Faery Queen* were animated by the mediaeval spirit.

> *Nought is more honourable to a knight*
> *Ne better doth beseem brave chivalry,*
> *Than to defend the feeble in their right,*
> *And wrong defend in such as wend awry;*
> *Whilom those great heroes got thereby*
> *Their greatest glory for their rightful deeds,*
> *And place deserved with the gods on high.*

The Red Cross Knight, who wore "the dear remembrance of his dying Lord," was "right, faithful, true, in deed and word," bent on great adventure, "to win him worship." Another noble warlike knight with well-deserved name

> *had filled far lands with glory of his might:*
> *Plain, faithful, true, and enemy of shame,*
> *And ever loved to fight for ladies' right.*

Truly chivalric are such remarks as: "mercy not withstand;" "all wrongs have mends, but no amends of shame;" "falsehood's foul attaint . . . all his other honour overthrew."

> *Fie on . . . forgery ! . . .*
> *Under one hood to shadow faces twain!*
> *Knights ought be true, and truth is one in all,*
> *Of all things to dissemble, foully may befall.*

And here, as in many other places, is the principle of fair play:

> *No knight so rude, I ween,*
> *As to do outrage to a sleeping ghost;*
> *Ne was there ever noble courage seen,*
> *That in advantage would his puissance boast:*
> *Honour is least where odds appeareth most.*

Spenser exalts the same knightly qualities as Malory, the same goodly temperance, stedfastness, and golden mean as are lauded in the *Order of Chivalry*. "Chivalry maketh thee to love wisdom," we read in the book just named; and "without temperance a knight may not maintain the order of chivalry, ne may not be in place where virtue dwelleth." By "wisdom's power and temperance's might," wrote Spenser, "the mightiest things enforced be." Wisdom and temperance, however, on Spenser's lips undoubtedly meant more than earlier met the ear. Old times had changed. The order of chivalry was rapidly giving way to what More called the order of the learned.

The more one studies Spenser's genius, the more one feels that, while he fully acknowledged the claims

of the Renaissance, his instinct persistently led him
to the Middle Ages. Mediaeval chivalric ideals were
fundamental in his system of conduct; but he deliberately united them with metaphysical conceptions
of moral principle, in association with which they
sometimes seem oppressed.

III

"In the person of Prince Arthur," the poet explains,
"I set forth magnificence in particular, which virtue, according to Aristotle, is the perfection of all
the rest." He conceives Arthur, "after his long education by Timon, to whom he was by Merlin delivered to be brought up, so soon as he was born of the
Lady Igrayne, to have seen in a vision the Faery
Queen, with whose excellent beauty ravished, he
awaking resolved to seek her out; and so, being by
Merlin armed, *and by Timon thoroughly instructed*,
he went to seek her forth in faeryland."

Arthur then is magnificence, the Faery Queen,
glory. The other virtues have other patrons " for the
more variety of the history." The first book tells
of the Red Cross Knight, expressing holiness; the
second of Sir Guyon, setting forth temperance ; the
third of Britomart, a lady knight, in whom is pictured
chastity. The ensuing books exemplify friendship
(Cambel and Triamond), justice (Sir Artegall), and
courtesy (Sir Calidore). There is also an unfinished

section on constancy. Here is certainly an elaborate
work, systematic, studied—a lordly, intellectual ven-
ture. The author himself terms it "a dark conceit."

Chaucer wrote tales for the sake primarily of the
tales, and his teaching is almost surreptitious. Malory wrote a corpus of romance which did not pre-
tend to be anything else; his personal remarks are
rare and incidental; one can almost pass them by
unobserved. But Spenser proclaims his mental purpose, as it were, with a trumpet from the house-top.
No one, he is determined, shall mistake his ambitious aim. He was not learned, cultivated, well-read,
for nothing. His goal, like Prince Arthur's, was the
kingdom of Gloriana. "Is aught on earth," asks one
of his heroes, "so precious or dear as praise and honour? Or is aught so bright and beautiful as glory's
beams appear?" Spenser's way to honour is by the
high road, not the obscure paths, of rightful deeds,
conspicuous for men to applaud. To deserve a place
with the gods on high it beseems one, he tells us,
to be virtuous; it behooves one to do well. He esteemed virtue the best policy. Public blame is his
great deterrent from idleness or vice.

Such sentiments are, indeed, far removed from
those of the *Imitation of Christ*. Read, by way of
contrast, what Thomas à Kempis says: "It is vanity
to hunt after honours." "Whoso knoweth himself
well, groweth more mean in his own conceit, and

delighteth not in the praises of men." "If thou wilt know or learn anything profitably, desire to be unknown, and to be little esteemed." We recognize that we have come into a new age, away from that of humble impersonality to that of superb individualism. We are considering a man who devoted himself to teaching posterity how to reach worldly fame, with the immediate object of increasing his own! Beside Spenser, Malory seems ingenuous, almost naïf, like Thomas à Kempis in the presence of Cardinal Wolsey, or Froissart before Machiavelli. Not self-suppression, but self-affirmation, animated Spenser's life. He was aware that he had

> *The noble heart that harbours virtuous thought,*
> *And is with child of glorious great intent.*

He could never rest until he brought forth "the eternal brood of glory excellent"—in this world!

Evidently Milton was questioning Spenserian ideas when, in *Lycidas*, he wrote:

> *Fame is the spur that the clear spirit doth raise*
> *(That last infirmity of noble mind)*
> *To scorn delights and live laborious days;*
> *But the fair guerdon when we hope to find,*
> *And think to burst out into sudden blaze,*
> *Comes the blind Fury with the abhorred shears,*
> *And slits the thin-spun life. . . .*
> *Fame is no plant that grows on mortal soil,*
> *Nor in the glistering foil*

Set off to the world, nor in broad rumour lies,
But lives and spreads aloft by those pure eyes
And perfect witness of all-judging Jove;
As he pronounces lastly on each deed,
Of so much fame in heaven *expect thy meed.*

Spenser had said: " Nothing is sure that grows on earthly ground;" but "broad-blazed fame," to be enjoyed here below, dazzled his eyes. He loved the sight of men "glistering in arms and battailous array," and loudly applauded those who sought the guerdon of glory on earth.

IV

"THE general end of all the [*Faery Queen*]," Spenser himself declared, was "to fashion a gentleman or noble person in virtuous and gentle discipline." Such words would never have proceeded from the mouth of Chaucer or Malory. "Discipline" is a word that Chaucer uses but once, in his translation of the Parson's Tale, and there of physical hardships only (like wearing a hair-shirt). Malory does not seem to use it at all. "Discipline " here signifies more than the outward precept or expert usage of earlier days: it insists on mental comprehension of underlying motive. "Virtue," moreover, has been impregnated with new intellectual significance in England since the fourteenth century. It resembles more the Italian *virtù*. "Virtue gives herself light through darkness for to wade."* The seat of this "virtue rare," Spenser affirms, is "deep within the mind." The word "mind," in truth, echoes and reëchoes throughout the *Faery Queen*. To the author assuredly, as to courtly Dyer, his mind a kingdom was, and there reason reigned in "due regality." Strong reason, Spenser declares, is what we must rely on to master frail passion. We should learn "lawless lust to rule with reason's lore." The fort of reason should be defended against the sore siege of strong affections. Even great grief should not make us forget "the reins to hold of reason's rule."

To be virtuous according to reason, we are instructed, demands constant self-consideration.* A man must not be lesser than himself. "Strive your excellent self to excel," writes the poet, "that shall ye evermore renowned make." The means is self-development, the end is renown! "Your acts are churlish" would have been Chaucer's keenest reproach; "You are no gentleman" would have been Malory's severest condemnation; "That is unworthy of you" epitomizes Spenser's blame.

> *The noble courage never weeneth aught*
> *That may unworthy of itself be thought.*

Virtue is "not in outward shows, but inward thoughts defined."

Spenser, who was inclined to be vague, and to see the past in "faint shadows of uncertain light," perhaps did not realize clearly that his emphasis on mental force in chivalry was new. Apostrophizing

the "goodly, golden chain, wherewith yfere the virtues linked are in lovely wise," he found them conspicuous in "noble minds of yore [who] allied were in
brave pursuit of chivalrous emprise." In his antique
age men "held virtue for herself in sovereign awe."

The poet's avowal that "gentle or noble persons"
were those whom he aimed to fashion by his les-
sons in the *Faery Queen*, points the way to Italy as
the chief source of what is new in his ideal of distinction. Spenser had evidently read with zest Castiglione's appealing *Book of the Courtier*, and had
fully assimilated its thought. First printed in 1528,
the *Courtier* "became an Englishman" through the
efforts of Sir Thomas Hoby in 1561, and was regarded then, as later by Dr. Johnson, as "the best
book that ever was written upon good breeding."
Sidney carried it always with him when he went
abroad.*

"Peradventure in all Italy," wrote the author, "a
man shall have much ado to find out so many *gentlemen and noble personages* that are so worthy and,
beside the *principal profession of chivalry,* so excellent
in sundry things as are presently here," at the court
of Urbino. It was to entertain and instruct similar
persons at the court of London that Spenser composed the *Faery Queen;* and, like Castiglione, he
began with the assumption that the "principal profession" of courtly gentlemen was chivalry.

It is curious to see how definitely the new Italian figure is a counterpart of Chaucer's Knight and Squire-son. He joins at different ages the sober virtues of the one with the brilliant accomplishments of the other. If to these we were also to add the intellectual attainments of the Clerk—a devotee of Aristotle and his philosophy, who spent his substance on books and learning, and had "moral virtue" ever on his lips—we should have the main essentials of the character. But while Chaucer outlined separate figures of a perfect Knight, Squire, and Clerk (as well as Parson), he did not attempt to picture what, in his time at least, did not exist, a perfect man, combining all the good qualities of each. Men of the Renaissance were more ambitious, if not more wise. Castiglione, reflecting that Plato had conceived in imagination a perfect commonweal, Xenophon a perfect king, and Cicero a perfect orator, undertook to describe a perfect "gentle and noble person," whom in his day it was reasonable to call a courtier. Before, no one had elaborately portrayed a "complete" man. Before, no one had thought of the courtier as the most likely individual to be ideally all-round.

Conditions, however, had so changed in England under Elizabeth that then the court was actually a focus of the highest aspiration. The Wars of the Roses had played havoc with the old nobility. New governmental policies had brought men of a new sort into the forefront of public life, men of talent rather than of birth, shrewd statesmen rather than bold warriors. One had come to applaud the endowments of nature and the ennoblements of the mind and genius, which should be, but were not necessarily, inherent in the blood and lineage.

Nor should we forget that—like Sidney, Raleigh, Bacon, and other prominent writers of his time—Spenser was himself a courtier. Court life was what he long desired for himself. But worldly fortune did not smile on him with the same benignity as the heavenly muse. He lived to be thoroughly disillusioned, and grew disgusted with the unchivalrous conduct of those in power. In his corrupted days, he felt, unlike "the antique use which was of yore," justice was "for meed outhired;" simple truth no longer reigned; "sunbright honour" was "penned in shameful coop." Though much went wrong at the English court, especially in Elizabeth's later years, it is probable that some of Spenser's bitterness was due to disappointment at his own failure to be exalted there.

In his satire entitled *Mother Hubberd's Tale,* pointing his shafts particularly at his foe, Lord Burleigh, the poet draws a long and acute contrast between the common courtier and the brave courtier. What the former loves and the latter loathes are clearly set forth. The rightful courtier, the courtly gentleman, among other things,

Will not creep, nor crouch with feigned face,
But walks upright with comely stedfast pace,
And unto all doth yield due courtesy. . . .
He hates foul leasings and vile flattery,
Two filthy blots in noble gentry;
And loathful idleness he doth detest,
The canker worm of every gentle breast.

He devises daily fair exercise, refreshes himself with music, and in quiet withdraws his mind unto the muses, "delights of life and ornaments of light." All his mind is fixed on honour. He spends his days in his prince's service, "to win worthy place through due deserts and comely carriage." At court, it is emphasized in the *Faery Queen,* vain shows are wont to bewitch young knights; being is better than seeming. The god Mammon is there with "idle offers of his golden fee;" one should not covet "eye-glutting gain."

Fie on the pelf for which good name is sold,
And honour with indignity debased,
Dearer is love than life, and fame than gold;
But dearer than them both your faith once plighted hold.

Such passages as these (and they might be multiplied) show the preoccupations of Spenser's mind.* He had enveloped himself with the refined atmosphere of Italian humanists and poets; yet, as an anxious Protestant, sympathizing at bottom with insular Anglo-Saxon moralists like Ascham and Cheke, he felt that his Italianate countrymen, of the Oxford-

Ormond-Hatton type, were open to the reproach of effeminacy and corruption. They had listened to the siren songs of "Circe's court." They sought too much their own advantage, not the welfare of the state. And he wrote with conviction the following manly lines:

> *Who-so in pomp of proud estate . . .*
> *Does swim and bathes himself in courtly bliss,*
> *Does waste his days in dark obscurity,*
> *And in oblivion ever buried is;*
> *Where ease abounds 't is eath to do amiss:*
> *But who his limbs with labours, and his mind*
> *Behaves with cares, cannot so easy miss.*
> *Abroad in arms, at home in studious kind,*
> *Who seeks with painful toil shall honour soonest find.*
>
> *In woods, in waves, in wars, she wonts to dwell,*
> *And will be found with peril and with pain;*
> *Ne can the man that moulds in idle cell*
> *Unto her happy mansion attain:*
> *Before her gate high God did sweat ordain,*
> *And wakeful watches ever to abide;*
> *But easy is the way and passage plain*
> *To pleasure's palace: it may soon be spied,*
> *And day and night her docrs to all stand open wide.*

In such a passage we hear rather the voice of Dante or Brunetto Latini than of any Italian of the sixteenth century.*

There was, however, another side to the story, which Spenser, quite as eagerly, wished no one to forget.

> *Of court, it seems, men courtesy do call,*
> *For that it there most useth to abound,*

> *And well beseemeth that in prince's hall*
> *That virtue should be plentifully found,*
> *Which of all goodly manners is the ground,*
> *And root of civil conversation.*

Goodly manners and civil conversation, it was the object of the *Courtier* to promote. Before Spenser, Castiglione perchance had heard the whispers of the Graces, "handmaids of Venus," "daughters of delight."

> *These three on men all gracious gifts bestow,*
> *Which deck the body or adorn the mind,*
> *To make them lovely or well-favoured show;*
> *As comely carriage, entertainment kind,*
> *Sweet semblaunt, friendly offices that bind,*
> *And all the complements of courtesy:*
> *They teach us how to each degree and kind*
> *We should ourselves demean, to low, to high,*
> *To friends, to foes; which skill men call civility.*

Milton ruminated with pleasure on Spenser's Graces —"daughters of sky-ruling Jove, . . . the first of them hight mild Euphrosyne"— and honoured him as "a better teacher than Scotus or Aquinas," but he openly demurs at the narrowness of Spenser's attitude, and in *Comus* commends

> *honest offered courtesy,*
> *Which oft is sooner found in lowly sheds*
> *With smoky rafters than in tapestry halls*
> *And courts of princes, where it first was named,*
> *And yet is most pretended.*

The recital of "wars, heroic deemed," was well enough, but there remained still, he thought, "the better fortitude of patience and heroic martyrdom unsung."

Spenser naturally believed that "peerless poesy" had its only fit home "in prince's palace." He wrote chiefly for a restricted circle. When at work in Ireland, he persistently yearned for the court of England, where, he deemed, were "happy peace and plenteous store, contented bliss"—as if these were calculated to quicken imaginative fire. In England, he then conceived:

> *The learned arts do flourish in great honour,*
> *And poets' wits are had in peerless price.*

Spenser was at his wit's end to see any merit in arts unlearned, in poetry unbidden or untaught—such was the short tether of his wit! He failed to confess to so great barbarousness as human Sidney, who never heard the old song of Percy and Douglas that he found not his heart moved more than with a trumpet. Spenser was not the poet of the careless brook or wayward mountain stream. He praised above all the springs of Helicon, while admitting the value of a moral mill-race and a gentle moat.

v

IN his day, the poet tells us, the very walls and windows of the English court were writ "all full of love, and love, my dear." The courtiers' whole talk and study was of love. Though this love was in the use of

many only an "idle name," "a compliment for court-
ing vain,"—not keeping them from lewd speeches
and licentious deeds,—it was nevertheless the result
of new acquaintance with philosophic thought on the
subject developed in the south. The following words
would have seemed strained to Chaucer, and they
would never have entered Malory's head at all:

> *Most sacred fire, that burnest mightily*
> *In living breasts, ykindled first above*
> *Amongst th' eternal spheres and lamping sky,*
> *And thence pour'd into men, which men call Love.*
> *Not that same, which doth base affections move*
> *In brutish minds, and filthy lust inflame,*
> *But that sweet fit that doth true beauty love,*
> *And chooseth virtue for his dearest dame,*
> *Whence spring all noble deeds and never dying fame.*

According to Spenser, three kinds of love often
together trouble the heart—to wit:

> *The dear affection unto kindred sweet,*
> *Or raging fire of love to womankind,*
> *Or zeal of friends combined with virtues meet.*

Yet of them all

> *the band of virtuous mind . . .*
> *. . . the gentle heart should most assured bind.*

> *For natural affection soon doth cease,*
> *And quenched is with Cupid's greater flame:*
> *But faithful friendship doth them both suppress,*
> *And them with mastering discipline doth tame;*
> *For as the soul doth rule the earthly mass,*
> *And all the service of the body frame,*

So love of soul doth love of body pass,
No less than perfect gold surmounts the meanest brass.

The subject of Platonism in Spenser might occupy us long. Ideas of Platonic love, drawn in part from Bembo's oration in the *Courtier*, are to be found throughout his work, most notably in *Epithalamium*, and the noble *Hymns to Love and Beauty*. These ideas are obviously not a natural fruit of French chivalry, but a graft from Greek philosophy.* Spenser, however, either failed to observe or deliberately obscured the difference. "*Throughout all ages,*" he says, "with the praise of arms and chivalry the praise of beauty has been joined," and that reasonably, "for either doth on other much rely." To him love was "the crown of knighthood," and he lingered joyfully over ancient tales in which, though simply, it was exhibited as such.

We have already seen how the poet repeated Chaucer's words on mastery in love. False Duessa seems to have had them in mind too when she says:

> *For love is free, and led with self delight,*
> *Ne will enforced be with masterdom or might.*

But her counsel to Sir Scudamour is so turned as to resemble that of the goose in the "*Fowls' Parley,*" at which the gentle birds took such offence:

> "*Nay, God forbede a lover shulde chaunge!*"
> *The turtel seyde, and wex for shame al reed;*

> *"Thogh that his lady ever more be straunge,*
> *Let him serve hir ever, til he be deed!"*

In mediaeval mood, Spenser also emphasized that it was better for a knight to die than to be false to his betrothed.

> *Unto knight there is no greater shame*
> *Than lightness and inconstancy in love.*
>
> *And ye, fair ladies, that your kingdom make,*
> *In th' hearts of men, them govern wisely well,*
> *And of fair Britomart ensample take,*
> *That was as true in love as turtle to her make.*
>
> *True love despiseth shame when life is called in dread.*

Like Chaucer, Spenser applauded stedfast loyalty and "faithful love, t' abide for evermore." Both poets exalted women full of grace and goodly modesty, who could wear such a magic girdle as that of Florimel, which gave to her it fitted "the virtue of chaste love and wifehood true;" both believed in wedlock's loyal bond. Continuing the Squire's Tale, Spenser makes fair Canacee and Triamond spend their days

> *In perfect love, devoid of hateful strife,*
> *Allied with bands of mutual complement.*

Like Dorigen to Arviragus, so Britomart to Artegall;

> *she yielded her consent*
> *To be his love, and take him for her lord.*
>
> *Love that two hearts make one, makes eek one will;*
> *Each strove to please, and other's pleasure to fulfil.*

The sort of love-relationship that Spenser thought wrong appears in his account of the Castle Joyous, with its marvellous Chamber of Ease.

> *And all was full of damsels and of squires,*
> *Dancing and revelling both day and night,*
> *And swimming deep in sensual desires;*
> *And Cupid still amongst them kindled lustful fires.*

The Red Cross Knight and Britomart, when they beheld the scene,

> *with scornful eye*
> *They [di]sdained such lascivious disport,*
> *And loath'd the loose demeanour of that wanton sort.*

They, like Spenser, abhorred such an one as Malecasta, the Lady of Delight. Though a creature of rare beauty, she had "wanton eyes, ill sign of womanhood." And Acrasia, who led many a knight by false enchantment to her Bower of Bliss, is termed vile. "Light ladies' love . . . soon is lost," says the poet. "As for loose loves, they're vain and vanish into naught." On the other hand, we have only to think of faithful Una, gracious Belphoebe, valiant Britomart, chaste Florimel, sweet Serena, gentle Amoret, affectionate Priscilla, or lovely Pastorella—all of them "fair" to the poet's eyes—to learn what ladies he would fain commend. Those fittest for their love were "wise, warlike, personable, courteous, and kind."

Evidently there was nothing Italianate in Spenser's view of passion. Idealistically he exalted Womanhood, and by her side in the Temple of Venus he placed goodly Shamefastness, sweet Cheerfulness, sober Modesty, comely Courtesy, soft Silence, and submissive Obedience—"in seemly rate." Spenser was thoroughly English in handling the problems of sex; but, beyond most of his countrymen, he proved able to disclose the gladdening power of sensuous charm; he succeeded in raising physical rapture without disquieting vile lust.

To unite pagan philosophy with Puritan morality, as Spenser did in his treatment of love, many view as a triumph of combination. They rejoice at the subtlety, the glory of his new teaching—sublimate and sublime. But others are stirred more deeply by the old winsome, unaffected emotion, true love, of which Spenser also felt the force, and delight most when he is inclined with simplicity to sing:

> *Love does always bring forth bounteous deeds,*
> *And in each gentle heart desire of honour breeds.*

> *Sweet is the love that comes alone with willingness.*

> *Truth is strong and true love most of might.*

VI

WHEN reading Spenser we think more of the sentiments the characters utter than of the characters themselves. Spenser's heroes and heroines are often too manifestly abstractions or allegorical figures to leave a distinct impression of personality. As one might expect, the despicable are more memorable than the virtuous: it seems much easier to individualize a sinner than a saint.

One of the best-remembered persons in the *Faery Queen* is the great boaster Braggadochio, who shows by contrast what a good knight should be.

> *Knight he was not, but a boastful swain,*
> *That deeds of arms had ever in despair,*
> *Proud Braggadochio, that in vaunting vain*
> *His glory did repose, and credit did maintain.*

Braggadochio was a "losell" peasant, who, purloining noble Guyon's steed and spear, thought to go to court and easily gain fame. "Vainglorious man!"

> *The scorn of knighthood and true chivalry,*
> *To think without desert of gentle deed*
> *And noble worth, to be advanced high.*

Never did he cast his mind to bounty; never did thought of honour assay his base breast. He was given to lust; he indulged in boastful vain pretence; he "left his love to loss."

There is much in this character that reminds one of Malory's King Mark. He too was false, mendacious, mean, a "self-loved personage" with a flowing tongue, a contemptible coward, who ran away from opponents with whom he feared to joust, one of whom all the world spoke shame—so unchivalric that he was finally dismissed from court in disgrace, stamped infamous yet the subject of jest.

When we see Braggadochio described as a peacock, a scarecrow, and consider his servant Trom-
part, a faithful and wily-witted knave, who upholds
the boaster's idle humour with flattery, and "blows
the bellows of his swelling vanity," a materialistic
creature fond of gold, who declares, whenever asked,
that he followed "a great adventurer, whose warlike name is far renowned through many bold emprise," yet was fully aware of his master's folly—
Don Quixote and Sancho Panza come to mind.

Braggadochio, however, unlike brave Don Quixote, cannot be regarded as a burlesque of knightly
excess, for the poet insists that he was merely a peasant counterfeit. Even if Spenser had so desired, he
had not humour enough to write a good burlesque.
In truth, there is ground to suspect that he took
Sir Thopas seriously. In his *State of Ireland*, the poet
gravely discussed Sir Thopas' apparel and armour
"when he went to fight against the giant," and compared it with that of Irish horsemen. The horsemanship of the Irish was one of the few attributes
of that people which he praised, and to judge by
the following passage, *à propos* of Braggadochio, his
praise was not lightly given:

> *In brave pursuit of honourable deed,*
> *There is I know not what great difference*
> *Between the vulgar and the noble seed,*
> *Which unto things of valorous pretence*
> *Seems to be borne by native influence;*

As feats of arms, and love to entertain:
But chiefly skill to ride seems a science
Proper to gentle blood: some other feign
To manage steeds, as did this vaunter, but in vain.

"Proper to gentle blood!" There were many other things besides skill to ride which Spenser felt that a gentleman should possess, and these he made plain, not only by indicating their absence in the vulgar, but also by applauding their presence in the noble seed.

Sir Calidore, than whom there is no more pleasing hero in the *Faery Queen*, perhaps best illustrates Spenser's view as to what qualities gentlemen ought to show. Sir Calidore was

beloved over-all,
In whom, it seems that gentleness of spirit
And manners mild were planted natural;
To which he adding comely guise withal
And gracious speech, did steal men's hearts away:

.   .   .   .

He loathed leasing and base flattery,
And loved simple truth and stedfast honesty.

This description recalls Malory's praise of Sir Gareth, though comely is a new adjective, and hatred of flattery a new attribute for him. Calidore in his travel meets Tristram, now an innocent youth, "Child Tristram," roaming the forests, clad like a woodman in Lincoln green, and sees him slay a proud discourteous knight, to save a lady from brutality. He remarks

that the boy's speech is "tempered" well, and that he
made answer with "poignant wit,"

> That sure he weened him born of gentle blood
> With whom those graces did so goodly fit.

From his face and "gracious goodlihed," the knight
concluded that Tristram was "surely born of some
heroic seed." He had won his battle worthily "by
his worth." Tristram is represented here, as in Malory, as a great lover of hunting, among his peers; but
it is new to learn of his tempered speech, his poignant
wit, his worthy worth.

Going on with his narrative, Spenser presently
quotes as true what "that good poet" Chaucer said,
but in another form: "The gentle mind by gentle
deeds is known," adding that "a man by nothing is
so well bewrayed as by his manners, in which plain
is shown of what degree and what race he is grown.
. . . Gentle blood will gentle manners breed." The
alteration of Chaucer's words is significant. Instead
of "he is gentle who doth gentle deeds," we read:
"The gentle *mind* by gentle deeds is known." But the
difference is more obvious in the remark: "Gentle
blood will gentle *manners* breed." Once again, when
Spenser returns to the same theme, he exclaims: "O
what an easy thing is to descry the gentle blood," for
no matter how foully deformed by misfortune, "yet
will it show some sparks of gentle *mind*, and at last

break forth in his own kind." Spenser lays the emphasis on gentle manners and gentle mind rather than on gentle deeds as the chief witnesses of gentle blood. He comes nearest Chaucer when he says:

> *The gentle* heart *itself bewrays*
> *In doing gentle deeds with frank delight.*

But he immediately shifts back to his more characteristic attitude when he adds:

> *Even so the baser* mind *itself displays*
> *In cancred malice and revengeful spite:*
> *For to malign, t' envy, t' use shifting slight,*
> *Be arguments of a vile, dunghill* mind.

Not without reason did Dr. Grosart dedicate his edition of Spenser to Lord Tennyson, "true child of that high race." The latter's words regarding Hallam betray at the end a like disposition to superiority:

> *So wore his outward best, and joined*
> *Each office of the social hour*
> *To noble manners, as the flower*
> *And native growth of noble mind;*
>
> *Nor ever narrowness or spite,*
> *Or villain fancy fleeting by,*
> *Drew in the expression of an eye,*
> *Where God and Nature met in light,*
>
> *And thus he bore without abuse*
> *The grand old name of gentleman,*
> *Defamed by every charlatan,*
> *And soiled with all ignoble use.*

It was natural, Spenser thought, that "wild woods

should far expel all civil usage and gentility and gentle sprite deform with rude rusticity." He assumed that court and royal citadel were the "great schoolmistress of all courtesy," that, therefore, one who had no skill of court nor courtesy was " a cancred crabbed carl." He wasted no sympathy on "the simple clown that doth despise the dainties of the town." He disdained rude churls, "brutishly brought up, that ne'er did fashions see." He contrasted the fair crew of brave knights and dainty dames with the baser crew, the rascal many, rude rablement, rustic rout, uncivil peasants, lewd fools, vile cowherd dogs. "Unto the vulgar," he declared, "forged things do fairest show"—"so feeble skill of perfect things the vulgar has!" Our thoughts wander back to Armado, Shakespeare's burlesque of men of Spenser's group. He too disdained the rude multitude. "O base and obscure vulgar!" he exclaimed: "we will be singled from the barbarous!" Spenser had admiration for his contemporaries who wrote plays, like Lyly, of a seemly sort; but he found repugnant those who were beginning to disguise "the fair scene with rudeness foul." They consorted, he thought, with "ugly barbarism and brutish ignorance," and with vain toys did "the vulgar entertain."

Spenser's considerations have regularly to do with what is fitting, what are one's duties to men of degree, what may keep one from courtly reproof of being rude, vulgar, barbarous, base—or (equally bad, perhaps) obscure! We are not surprised to have him begin one canto of the *Faery Queen* with this apostrophe:

> *Redoubted knights and honourable dames,*
> *To whom I level all my labour's end.*

He believed that the "nobility" were "the realm's chief strength and garland of the crown."

But who, we may ask, formed this "nobility"? Evidently, "noble and gentle persons," persons of quality, measured by the standards of the *Courtier*. Though Spenser agreed with Castiglione that it was a condition of a perfect noble person "to be well-born and of a good stock," he too was willing to admit exceptions to the rule:

> *Certes, it hath oftentimes been seen,*
> *That of the like, whose lineage was unknown,*
> *More brave and noble knights have raised been*
> *(As their victorious deeds have often shown,*
> *Being with fame through many nations blown)*
> *Than those which have been dandled in the lap:*
> *Therefore some thought that those brave imps were sown*
> *Here by the gods, and fed with heavenly sap,*
> *That made them grow so light t' all honourable hap.*

These last sound very much like Castiglione's words: "Truth it is, whether it be thought the favour of the stars or of nature, some there are born endowed with such graces, that they seem not to have been born, but rather fashioned with the very hand of some god, and abound in all goodness both of body and mind."

Castiglione briefly states his views of nobility as follows: " It is a great deal less dispraise for him that is not born a gentleman to fail in the acts of virtue than for a gentleman. If he swerve from the steps of his ancestors, he staineth the name of his family, and doth not only not get, but loseth that is already gotten. For nobleness of birth is, as it were, a clear lamp that sheweth forth and bringeth into light works both good and bad, and enflameth and provoketh unto virtue, as well with the fear of slander, as also with the hope of praise."

Such considerations had evoked others similar in England before Spenser wrote. In an interesting chapter of his *Book named the Governor* (1531), Sir Thomas Elyot discusses "what very nobility is" and who are "noble persons," and emphasizes that noble "signifieth excellent, and in the analogy or signification it is more ample than gentle, for it containeth as well all that which is in gentleness, as also the honour or dignity therefore received, which be so annexed the one to the other that they cannot be separate." "It would be moreover declared," he adds, "that where virtue joined with great possessions or dignity hath long continued in the blood or house of a gentleman, as it were an inheritance, there nobility is most shewed, and these noble men be most to be honoured; forasmuch as continuance in all thing that is good hath ever preëminence in praise and comparison. But yet shall it be necessary to advertise [warn] those persons that do think that nobility may in no wise be but only where men can avaunt them of ancient lineage, an ancient robe, or great possessions, at this day very noble men do suppose to be much error and folly. . . . Nobility is not after the vulgar opinion of men, but is only the praise and surname of virtue; which, the longer it continueth in a name or lineage, the more is nobility extolled and marvelled at."

In sixteenth-century England, scholars concerned themselves more with the principles of nobility than with the laws of chivalry; but with men of action it was the reverse. Spenser, happily, had before him as a pattern of manhood one who was "president" (precedent) of both "noblesse and chivalry," and in the *Faery Queen* he entered all his thoughts on virtue, wherever derived.

Spenser's living ideal was Sir Philip Sidney, and that noble and virtuous gentleman he describes as "most worthy of all titles both of learning and chivalry." In the combination of learning and chivalry lay the secret of the Italian ideal which stirred these friends to their distinction. "Beside goodness," wrote Castiglione, "the true and principal ornament of the mind in every man are letters. The Frenchmen know

only the nobleness of arms, and pass for nothing beside. So that they do not only not set by letters, but
they rather abhor them, and all learned men they
count very rascals and think it is a great villainy when
any of them is called a clerk." Perhaps with this passage before him, Peacham, in the seventeenth century, remarked again: "They [the French nobility]
delight for the most part in horsemanship, fencing,
hunting, dancing, and little esteem of learning and
gifts of the mind." If this was really the case, it was
not because efforts had not been made earlier in
France herself to alter it. Alain Chartier protests in
his poem *Espérance:** "Fol langage court aujour-
d'hui que noble homme ne doit savoir les lettres.*" And
Christine de Pisan (if, indeed, she is the author) thus
opens her admirable Life of Boucicaut: "Two things
are, by the will of God, established in the world, like
two pillars to sustain the orders of divine and human
laws, which give rule to human weakness to live in
peace, and duly under the terms of reason, and
which increase and multiply human sense in knowledge and virtue and remove its ignorance. . . . These
two pillars are chivalry and learning, which very well
agree together." Most noteworthy is Christine's description of her admirable hero: "*Lequel dit chevalier
fut moult preud'omme et de grand savoir.*" St. Louis
was more than content to be a *preud'omme* alone.

With others like-minded and like-trained, Chris-

tine strove in France to effect a union of learning
and chivalry, but plainly with less success than was
achieved beyond the Alps. The same situation con-
fronts us in England. Despite all the urgings of Spenser and his group, the majority of English knights
seem to have remained as undisturbed by their in-
completeness as the French. Skelton had said in *Colin
Clout:*

> *Noble men born,*
> *To learn they have scorn,*
> *But hunt and blow an horn,*
> *Leap over lakes and dikes,*
> *Set nothing by polytykes.*

Sir Humphrey Gilbert closes his plea for the institution to be called "Queen Elizabeth's Academy,"
with equal frankness: "By erecting this Academy,
there shall be hereafter in effect no gentleman within
this realm but is good for somewhat, whereas now
the most part of them are good for nothing. And yet
thereby the court shall not only be greatly increased
with gallant gentlemen, but also with men of virtue,
whereby Your Majesty's and successors' courts shall
be forever, instead of a nursery of idleness, a most
noble academy of chivalric policy and philosophy, to
your great fame."

In Queen Elizabeth's age chivalry was still a name
to conjure with. When Peacham wrote, in 1634,*
he naturally substituted for it "the fear of God;"
but the Renaissance plea for learning he proudly re-

newed: "Since *learning joined with the fear of God*
is so faithful a guide that without it princes undergo
but lamely (as Chrysostom saith) their greatest affairs—they are rude in discretion, ignorant in knowledge, rude and barbarous in manners and living—
the necessity of it in princes and nobility may easily
be gathered, who, howsoever they flatter themselves
with the favourable sunshine of their great estates and
fortunes, are indeed of no other account and reckoning with men of wisdom and understanding than
glowworms that only shine in the dark of ignorance
and are admired of idiots and the vulgar for the outside, statues or huge colossos full of lead and rubbish
within."

This lack of learning among men of rank has been
steadily bewailed by scholars to our own day. Their
laments might have been more effective (they would
certainly have been more worthy) had they not exhibited so often the superciliousness of bookish snobs
—ugly "vileinye" of a sort that no perfect, gentle
knight would address to any fellow man. From grievous words of disdain Spenser was not free. He states
his own attitude thus: "The better please, the worse
despise, I ask no more."

It is very gratifying, on the contrary, to find the
poet hesitate to use the word "scorn" of Sir Philip
Sidney, because, he said, it was not "in the goodness of that nature to scorn." Sidney's character was

grounded on the very noble, but very difficult, ideal
of Christian chivalry, which demanded that a man
should strive to make himself beloved. The most
marvellous thing, indeed, about that gentle knight
is that from all sorts of persons, high and low, as his
father witnessed, he won love. He must have been, as
Shelley thought, "sublimely mild."

> *He grew up fast in goodness and in grace,*
> *And doubly fair wox both in mind and face,*
> *Which daily more and more he did augment,*
> *With gentle usage and demeanour mild:*
> *That all men's hearts with secret ravishment*
> *He stole away, and wittingly beguiled.*
> *Ne spite herself, that all good things doth spill,*
> *Found aught in him that she could say was ill.*

Sidney, as Fulke Greville wrote, was "a true
model of worth; a man fit for conquest, plantation,
reformation, or what action soever is greatest and
hardest among men; withal such *a lover of mankind*
and goodness, that whosoever had any real parts,
in him found comfort, participation and protection
to the uttermost of his power. . . . [He was] the
common rendez-vous of worth in his time." "True
worth," which meant to Sidney "esteeming fame
more than riches, and noble actions far above nobility itself," is the finest note of the conception of
chivalry that Spenser presents. Great, heroic, noble,
wondrous, famous, knightly, are all adjectives he
joins to worth. Chaucer admired the Black Prince,

"the flower of chivalry;" Malory, the Earl of Warwick, "father of courtesy;" Spenser, Sir Philip Sidney, "worthy of all titles both of learning and chivalry," apostle and mirror of worth. Sir Philip Sidney,
we can all acclaim without reserve—true "lover of
mankind."

Spenser was a poet of "liberal" education and culture. Of the four writers here particularly considered,
he was the only one who was a university man, or
had the ideals, as well as the prejudices, that still prevail at Oxford and Cambridge, comparatively little
changed from the poet's time. Graduates of these
colleges—"England's goodly beams"—have long
cherished the idea that they formed a select body of
"noble or gentle persons," preëminently fitted by reason of their "virtuous and gentle discipline" to set
standards in the nation and direct its affairs. Most
have been zealous "to join learning with comely exercises," and many have sought in public life to en-
hance their country's honour. When true to themselves as "gentlemen and scholars," they have acted
with dignity and self-control; they have spoken with
well-tempered speech, and rebuked unseemly demeanour. Recognizing that intellectual as well as
hereditary *noblesse* has obligations, the best have
laboured to confirm the old belief: *Abeunt studia in
mores*. Because "manners," thus founded, still make

men, Englishmen are still deeply indebted to all
who advanced the lofty ideals of conduct elaborated
in the Renaissance, to none more, despite his faults,
than to Edmund Spenser, who joined "seraphic intel-
lect . . . and manhood fused with female grace," a

High nature, amorous of the good,
But touched with no ascetic gloom.

SHAKESPEARE

SHAKESPEARE

IN England, before Spenser died, feudalism had lost its force; more and more the monarchy was to be limited and the commoner to become distinguished in the realm. Catholicism, as an institution, had then succumbed before violent attack; henceforth Protestants alone were to occupy the throne and rule the Established Church. Scholasticism had reluctantly recoiled before the onslaught of humanists; collegiate discipline was to be increasingly broadened by new science. Parochialism, after long waiting, had ceased to characterize English speech; few Englishmen in the future were to write Latin or French; fate promised universality to the mother-tongue. Nationalism had at last stirred the hearts of men of every rank, and writers had appeared in whom all English-speaking peoples will forever rejoice. One had come who far surpasses every other of his countrymen in wide renown.

Shakespeare was born eleven years after Spenser, and survived him by seventeen. For thirty-five years both lived under the same sovereign, with their eyes on the same court. Yet there was a social gulf between them. The one was an ambitious suitor to Elizabeth for offices of note; the other gained humble success acting at her command. The one wrote for the applause of refined circles, and associated on intimate terms with distinguished nobles; the other, though he had a great patron and close acquaintances among the aristocracy, made a business of purveying plays to the general public, and appearing in them for pecuniary gain, "a motley to the view." If it be Shakespeare to whom Spenser refers as Aetion in *Colin Clout*, he praised him merely as a writer of elaborate lyric verse.

> *And there, though last not least, is Aetion;*
> *A gentler shepherd may nowhere be found,*
> *Whose muse, full of high thought's invention,*
> *Doth like himself heroically sound.*

Shakespeare had just begun his poetic career when the following words appeared in the *Faery Queen*:

> *Gold all is not that doth golden seem;*
> *Ne all good knights that* shake *well* speare *and shield.*
> *The worth of all men by their end esteem,*
> *And then due praise or due reproach him yield.*

It would perhaps be fanciful to find here another reference to Spenser's coming rival; but we may accept the thought of the passage, and, having the whole wonderful Folio whereby to judge, unhesitatingly declare Shakespeare's worth, as he did that of the hero of his sonnets, "a limit past [our] praise."

Shakespeare is a far greater marvel than Spenser, not only on account of the gift of a loftier genius, but also because his attainments more fully belied the circumstances of his early environment and education. It passes understanding how he should have had the wise "skill in discourse" which he himself conceived in his beloved Henry V, and been able to frame such "sweet and honey'd sentences" as distinguish his many works,

> *Since his addiction was to courses vain;*
> *His companies unletter'd, rude, and shallow;*
> *His hours fill'd up with riots, banquets, sports;*
> *And never rooted in him any study,*
> *Any retirement, any sequestration*
> *From open haunts and popularity.*

Still "the strawberry grows underneath the nettle," and Shakespeare's human greatness may have been partly due to his necessary acquaintance with unveiled nature, with artless life. Had he been brought up to privilege, he might not have had the same spur to achievement; had he been university-bred, he might not have so widely shunned pedantry and pose; had he lived secluded, he might have failed to touch the chords of all humanity.

Shakespeare's character and tastes we must in the main divine from the evidence of his work, and no one can be infallible in such divination. Still, this at least is clear: meditation upon his own place in society and personal distinction dominates some of his most poignant sonnets, and, if these are in any way autobiographical, the author regretted the misfortune of his stars. He would fain have boasted a "proud

title," experienced "public honour," and been "with
friends possess'd." All alone he bewept his "outcast
state;" he sighed the lack of many a thing he sought.
He was of the purest blood royal of poets, and
endowed with riches of the imagination surpassing
all the high-born whom he admired, yet with what
he "most possessed" he was "contented least." Fortune "did not better for [his] life provide than public means, which public manners breeds." "In sleep
a king, but waking no such matter"! The outer
facts of Shakespeare's life show steady desire on his
part to improve his social position. He cultivated a
noble patron, and became his affectionate friend.
He strove for wealth, and secured a landed estate.
Though a poor tradesman's son, he made himself
a leading citizen of his native town, and was le-
gally granted admittance to the gentry—"*non sanz
droict.*"

Shakespeare seems to have been endowed by nature with personal grace. His comrades spoke of his
"civil demeanour;" they noted his sweetness, uprightness, and honesty, his "open and free nature;" they
called his expressions, his verse, and him himself, by
his own favourite term of commendation, "gentle."
What though he had no great old "household coat,"
he had still, like exiled Bolingbroke, the sign of
"men's opinions and [his] living blood to show the
world [he was] a gentleman." He was, in truth, still

more. We may confidently say of him, as Antony
did of noble Brutus:

> *His life was gentle, and the elements*
> *So mix'd in him that Nature might stand up*
> *And say to all the world: "This was a man"!*

"I loved the man," said Ben Jonson, "and do honour his memory on this side idolatry, as much as any."

> *My Shakespeare, rise! I will not lodge thee by*
> *Chaucer, or Spenser, or bid Beaumont lie*
> *A little farther off to make thee room:*
> *Thou art a monument without a tomb,*
> *And art alive still, while thy book doth live,*
> *And we have wits to read and praise to give.*

I

SHAKESPEARE's first published works were *Venus
and Adonis* and *The Rape of Lucrece*. Evidently, it
was by what he calls "gentle verse," not by plays,
that he expected to win recognition in the world of
the great.

Though the rape of Lucrece was a classical theme,
Chaucer's version of the story was accessible to the
poet, and it is important to observe how he allowed
mediaeval sentiments to adhere to his own. We have
seen, from a passage earlier quoted, that Chaucer
indignantly apostrophized Tarquin for having done
a villain's deed, "despite to chivalry," which was
much the worse because of his royal birth. In similar
fashion, Shakespeare's Lucrece importunes him to

believe that since he is a king, a lustful act would bring him peculiar shame. She conjures him by "knighthood and gentry," as well as by other oaths. Later, when telling her story, she requires each of the fair lords before her to plight his honourable faith to revenge her on the traitor, since "knights by their oaths should right poor ladies' harms." Each of them at once promises her his aid, "as bound in knighthood." Still more striking is the passage where Tarquin, premeditating his deed, breaks out as follows:

> *O shame to knighthood and to shining arms!*
>
> *Yea, though I die, the scandal will survive,*
> *And be an eyesore in my golden coat;*
> *Some loathsome dash the herald will contrive,*
> *To cipher me how fondly I did dote;*
> *That my posterity, sham'd with the note,*
> *Shall curse my bones, and hold it for no sin*
> *To wish that I their father had not been.*

Chaucer lived before the Herald's College had been founded; but Shakespeare knew all about it, even to its "dashes," or abatements, for dishonour. He himself was then seeking a golden coat to dignify his posterity. He makes Tarquin of Rome echo his personal preoccupation with the advantage it would procure. He even analyzes the "heraldry" in his heroine's face.

For *Troilus and Cressida*, as for *Lucrece*, Shakespeare had the example of Chaucer, and for *Pericles* that of Gower, so that he was naturally disposed to fill these plays with feudal anachronisms, as his predecessors had filled their poems on the same themes. *King Lear* and *Cymbeline* dealt ostensibly with events in ancient Britain, and, since it had been the regular custom throughout the Middle Ages for those who rehandled Celtic tales to reflect in so doing the circumstances of their own time, it is not surprising to find in Shakespeare's treatment a large infusion of mediaeval as well as modern thought. But, in truth, we find nearly everywhere in the poet's productions knightly conceptions influencing his standards of right, and frequently old images of romance suggesting his turns of phrase.

Shakespeare, it should not be forgotten, was obliged to make a close study of the age of chivalry before being able to write his historical works. Of these *King John*, *Richard II*, the two parts of *Henry IV*, *Henry V*, the three parts of *Henry VI*, and *Richard III*—nine plays, all written before he had reached middle life—concern themselves with a period when chivalry was a living force, and it would have been impossible for anyone to picture properly the courtly events of that time and not hold the mirror up to knightly practice and sentiment. The facts, first, that Shakespeare chose to write these plays, and then, that he described the scenes of mediaeval life therein contained with glad zest, sufficiently attest his sympathy for that lofty manner of envisaging duty which illumines the epoch with a splendid light. Edward Kirke, when defending Spenser's use of archaic words, pointed out that it was natural for him, being "much travelled and thoroughly read" in the ancient English poets, to have their sounds "still ringing in his ears," so that he "must needs in singing hit out some of their tunes." It was, he declares, as Cicero said: "Walking in the sun, although for other cause he walked, yet needs he must be sunburnt." This is exactly Shakespeare's situation. He walked cheerfully and long in the open air of the Middle Ages, and his whole face was tanned by the sun of chivalry.

II

MANY outer features of chivalric life naturally appear in the poet's plays. Often, for example, he refers to the dubbing of knights, laying particular emphasis on this honour when done before, during, or after a battle, as a stimulant to courage. Robert Faulconbridge was knighted "by the honour-giving hand of Cœur-de-lion . . . in the field." His bastard son, Philip, was dubbed by King John while preparing for a war in France. Henry V promised before Agincourt that that day would "gentle the condition" of those who shed their blood with him; they should be his

brothers. When a herald gave him the numbers of
the French who were slain in this conflict, he remarked: "Five hundred were but yesterday dubbed
knights." The stalwart esquire, Alexander Iden, who
slew the rebel Cade, was knighted by his sovereign
for " good service;" and Henry VI, at the queen's
request, dubbed his own son:

> Edward Plantagenet, arise a knight;
> And learn this lesson, draw thy sword in right.

Once dubbed, the knight had above all to defend
his honour, which sometimes led him to demand a
trial by combat to settle a dispute with another person of similar rank. *Richard II* begins with an appeal to the king for such a contest of strength. Henry
Bolingbroke, afterwards Henry IV, accuses Thomas
Mowbray of high treason, and begs to be allowed to
prove by his sword that what he says is true. Finally
he throws down his "gage," his "honour's pawn," to
show thereby "and all the rites of knighthood else,"
that he will make good his words. Mowbray replies:

> I take it up; and by that sword I swear,
> Which gently laid my knighthood on my shoulder,
> I'll answer thee in any fair degree
> Or chivalrous design of knightly trial.

He denounces Bolingbroke as a "foul liar," while he
undertakes "to prove [himself] a loyal gentleman."
The king and John of Gaunt endeavour to make
peace between the two, but in vain; both refuse to

let anyone command their "shame." Naught availing
otherwise, they are bidden to appear at Coventry on
St. Lambert's Day, when the "victor's chivalry" will
reveal the right. On the day appointed, the lists are
arranged, and all proceeds in due order. The marshal
demands public statement of his cause on the part
of each champion, and makes him swear to its justice
on the sacred oath of knighthood, "which God defend
a knight should violate." They bid their friends a solemn farewell. Heralds proclaim that each is ready,
"on pain to be found false and recreant," to prove
his adversary traitorous or disloyal. The combatants
are on the point of setting forward. But—"Stay! the
king has thrown his warder down." He forbids the
combat; he proclaims the banishment of both. Of
other scenes of the same sort, the most notable is that
near the end of *King Lear*, where we have a trial by
combat executed in the manner of the fourteenth
century. Openly before the court, the heroic Edgar
proclaims his half-brother Edmund "a most toad-
spotted traitor."

> *Say thou,* No,
> *This sword, this arm, and my best spirits, are bent*
> *To prove upon thy heart, whereto I speak,*
> *Thou liest.*

Edmund, scorning to take advantage of the rule of
knighthood which excused him from fighting "an
unknown opposite," repudiates the accusation of trea-

son, and tosses back to his enemy "the hell-hated lie." Edgar wins, strong in a righteous cause.

A less serious, but equally characteristic, chivalric situation occurs in *Pericles*, where the poet describes a great assembly whither knights have come from all parts of the world, "for honour's cause," to joust for the love of King Simonides' daughter. Though in appearance a "mean knight," Pericles of Tyre wins the prize handsomely, whereupon the princess gives him the wreath of victory, and crowns him "king of this day's happiness." It is not without significance that this tournament was substituted by Shakespeare for a ball-game in his source.

In *Cymbeline* the plot hinges on the readiness of a valiant hero to fight for his lady's name. Posthumus, when abroad in youth, had been prepared to prove by his sword that his lady was "more fair, virtuous, wise, chaste, constant-qualified, and less attemptable" than the rarest in France; and he is willing to accept Iachimo's challenge to test Imogen's honour, on the covenant that, if the plan fail, the Italian shall answer for his ill-opinion in a duel. To judge from the autobiography of Lord Herbert of Cherbury, such an occurrence was not infrequent in Shakespeare's own day among men who clung to knightly practices. On one occasion, Lord Herbert relates: "Being among the French, I remembered myself of the bravado of Monsieur Balagny, and coming to him told him, I knew how brave a man he was, and that as he had put me to one trial of daring, when I was last with him in the trenches, I would put him to another; saying, I heard he had a fair mistress, and that the scarf he wore was her gift, and that I would maintain I had a worthier mistress than he, and that I would do as much for her sake as he or anyone else durst do for his." To this Balagny made a coarse reply, and the earnest Englishman, "looking hereupon somewhat disdainfully on him, said he spoke more like a *paillard* than a cavalier." Lord Herbert tells us that he took seriously the vows he made when initiated a Knight of the Bath, observing that certain of these—for example, "never to sit in place where injustice should be done, but they shall right it to the uttermost of their power; and particularly ladies and gentlemen that shall be wronged in their honour, if they demand assistance" —were "not unlike the romances of knight-errantry." He loved to regard himself in a chivalric light, and laid particular stress on his many duels fought (rather too self-consciously) in the name of honour. Some of these duels were so famous in England that Shakespeare must have heard them discussed, particularly since Lord Herbert belonged to the circle of the Earl of Southampton, and was intimate with Sir Thomas Lucy of Charlecote, near Stratford-on-Avon.

One of Lord Herbert's most spectacular performances occurred in the Netherlands when he was serving the Prince of Orange. He was then bold enough to send a trumpeter to the camp of the opposing army of Spain, to challenge any Spanish soldier to meet him before the hosts and to "fight a single combat for the sake of his mistress." This incident is curiously parallel to that in *Troilus and Cressida*, when Aeneas comes as herald to the Greeks and challenges some one of them to meet Hector alone in arms.

> *If there be one amongst the fair'st of Greece*
> *That holds his honour higher than his ease,*
> *That seeks his praise more than he fears his peril,*
> *That knows his valour, and knows not his fear,*
> *That loves his mistress more than in confession*
> *. . . to him this challenge.*
> *Hector, in view of Troyans and of Greeks,*
> *Shall make it good, or do his best to do it.*
> *He hath a lady, wiser, fairer, truer,*
> *Than ever Greek did compass in his arms.*

It is odd to hear Agamemnon, when he promises to bear Hector's message to the Greek "lovers," voice this mediaeval sentiment: "May that soldier a mere recreant prove, that means not, hath not, or is not in love." It is equally odd for old Nestor (who was a man "when Hector's grandsire suck'd") to be stirred by the challenge, and to undertake to hide his silver beard in a gold beaver and put his withered brawn in his vantbrace to prove that his "lady" is fair and chaste. Nestor in mediaeval armour fighting in the lists for his lady! In the ensuing conflict Diomed wears on his helmet Cressida's "sleeve," which once had belonged to Troilus, and when he sends the latter's horse to her, commends his "service;" he has "chastis'd the amorous Troyan," and is "her knight by proof."

With such anachronisms in *Troilus*, it is not strange to find there also a discussion of fair play.* Troilus, though a "prince of chivalry," becomes so wild when he learns of Cressida's infidelity, that he begins this unworthy conversation with Hector, and meets a merited rebuke:

TROILUS. *Brother, you have a vice of mercy in you,*
Which better fits a lion than a man.
HECTOR. *What vice is that, good Troilus? Chide me for it.*
TROILUS. *When many times the captive Grecian falls,*
Even in the fan and wind of your fair sword,
You bid them rise and live.
HECTOR. *O, 'tis fair play.*
TROILUS. *Fool's play, by heaven, Hector!*

.   .   .   .

HECTOR. *Fie, savage, fie.*

Hector, however, is shown the opposite of fair play by Achilles. After the last great battle, believing himself alone on the field, the hero takes off his helmet and hangs his shield behind him. Then Achilles approaches suddenly, and, even though Hector makes appeal: "I am unarm'd: forego this vantage, Greek,"

bids his myrmidons strike. Still more! The murderer
ties Hector's body to his horse's tail "in beastly sort,"
and trails it "through the shameful field." This conduct was so vile that even Ajax broke out when he
heard the news:

> *If it be so, yet bragless let it be;*
> *Great Hector was a man as good as he.*

Hector was "worthy," and it was wholly "i' the vein
of chivalry" that he avowed:

> *Mine honour keeps the weather of my fate.*
> *Life every man holds dear; but the dear man*
> *Holds honour far more precious-dear than life.*

III

"THERE are," wrote Hallam, "if I may so say, three
powerful spirits which have from time to time moved
over the face of the waters, and given a predominant
impulse to the moral sentiments and energies of mankind. These are the spirits of liberty, of religion, and
of honour. It was the principal business of chivalry to
animate and cherish the last of these three. And whatever high magnanimous energy the love of liberty
or religious zeal has ever imparted was equalled by
the exquisite sense of honour which this institution
preserved."

Nothing attests more convincingly the power that
chivalric ideals had over Shakespeare than his constant insistence on honour. The word occurs through-

out his plays. He seems hardly to have been able to conceive a great man of action save in a chivalric light. While we are not surprised to have a mediae-val English king like Henry V declare that he is not "covetous for gold" or fine garments, but that "if it be a sin to covet honour," he is "the most offend-ing soul alive," we do not look for such sentiments from warriors of Rome. Shakespeare, nevertheless, represents Antony as brooding on his honour, which called him from Cleopatra, who had caught him " in her strong toil of grace," and puts into the mouth of Enobarbus memorable words on loyalty:

> *The loyalty well held to fools does make*
> *Our faith mere folly: — yet he that can endure*
> *To follow with allegiance a fallen lord,*
> *Does conquer him that did his master conquer*
> *And earns a place i' the story.*

Still more remarkable is the way in which the poet pictures Brutus as "a very perfect gentle knight." Brutus, indeed, measures up, as much as any of Shakespeare's characters, to the standard of Chaucer's pattern of worthiness. When Cassius comes to incite him to oppose Caesar, the hero declares:

> *If it be aught toward the general good,*
> *Set honour in one eye, and death i' the other,*
> *And I will look on both indifferently;*
> *For, let the gods so speed me as I love*
> *The name of honour more than I fear death.*

"Well," replies Cassius, "honour is the subject of

my story;" and, after they have parted, he exclaims: "Brutus, thou art noble!" Casca, too, remarks on his leader's nobility and its effect:

> *O, he sits high in all the people's hearts;*
> *And that which would appear offence in us,*
> *His countenance, like richest alchemy,*
> *Will change to virtue and to worthiness.*

Brutus will not demand oaths of his fellow conspirators; he thinks they need no other bond than to have "spoke the word," no other oath than "honesty to honesty engaged." He admonishes his "gentle friends" to kill Caesar boldly, but not wrathfully; he desires that they shall be called "purgers, not murderers;" for theirs was an "exploit worthy the name of honour." In his address to the people, Brutus pleads: "Believe me for mine honour; and have respect to mine honour that ye may believe." Antony, in his famous speech of mourning, plays on this, his friend's sensitive point:

> *Brutus is an honourable man;*
> *So are they all, all honourable men.*

And he puts the case so craftily (dwelling on the "gracious drops" of pity) that the citizens, previously ready to accept the situation because of their confidence in Brutus, break out scornfully, in words that evince an old-time knightly contrast:

> *They were traitors;* honourable men! . . .
> *They were villains, murderers.*

Brutus was "noble, wise, valiant and honest." He accepted the grievous blow of his wife's death with patience, not of art, but nature; "even so great men great losses should endure!"

There was probably self-deception in Brutus' persuasion that pure honour guided his conduct toward Caesar, and this may explain why, when meditating on the plot, the hero cast "ungentle looks" at Portia, and exhibited impatient anger in her presence. Portia observed that he was not then himself, "*gentle* Brutus." She was "true and honourable," and it was perhaps more than fear of feminine indiscretion that made her husband refrain from taking her at once into his confidence. His noble mind had been seduced, and he was apparently too well aware of the purity of Portia's sense of honour to be willing to submit his dubious scheme to her scrutiny. "There are no tricks," he knew, "in plain and simple faith."

In the *Merchant of Venice* Shakespeare described another Portia, "nothing undervalued to Cato's daughter," who also cherished honour. Into this Portia's mouth the poet put his magnificent exaltation of mercy, "mighty in the mightiest," which quality, along with that other chivalric one, pity, the Jew Shylock so glaringly lacked. Unlike "stubborn Turks and Tartars, never train'd to offices of tender courtesy," Antonio and Bassanio were genuine patterns

of "ancient Roman honour," differing in no respect
from that of Christian England and France. Antonio, at the beginning of the play, shows himself willing to serve his friend to the extreme of his means,
"if it stand . . . within the eye of honour," and at
the end he dares be bound upon his soul's forfeit that
the same friend will never in the future "break faith
advisedly." Bassanio's honour would not let ingrati-
tude "besmear" it; he was willing to sacrifice all
that he held as dear as life, even life itself, to show
Antonio becoming loyalty.

> *Who shall go about*
> *To cozen fortune, and be honourable*
> *Without the stamp of merit? Let none presume*
> *To wear an undeserved dignity.*
> *O, that estates, degrees and offices*
> *Were not deriv'd corruptly! And that clear honour*
> *Were purchas'd by the merit of the wearer!*
> *How many then should cover that stand bare!*
> *How many be commanded that command!*
> *How much low peasantry would then be glean'd*
> *From the true seed of honour! and how much honour*
> *Pick'd from the chaff and ruin of the times*
> *To be new-varnish'd!*

When writing these lines, Shakespeare's thought was
centred on conditions in England rather than in Ar-
ragon or Italy, and in exalting clear honour purchased
by the merit of the wearer, he showed kinship in attitude with the greatest earlier poets of his land. Even
so it was with his glorification of mercy.

Wilt thou draw near the nature of the gods?
Draw near them then in being merciful.
Sweet mercy is nobility's true badge.

In *2 Henry VI*, the poet proclaims, as Sidney felt, that a knight's heart should accord with his tongue, and adds:

What stronger breastplate than a heart untainted;
Thrice is he arm'd that hath his quarrel just,
And he but naked, though lock'd up in steel,
Whose conscience with injustice is corrupted.

Apart from the chivalric thought in this passage, one is struck by the figures of its expression, drawn as they are from knightly accoutrement. Such figures are frequent in Shakespeare. We read, for example, of "grey locks, the poursuivants of death." Hotspur does not desire, when war is brewing, to "tilt with lips." Macbeth exclaims:

Come fate into the list,
And champion me to the utterance!

The Earl of Salisbury observes of King John:

The colour of the king doth come and go
Between his purpose and his conscience,
Like heralds 'twixt two dreadful battles set.

Shakespeare shows his absorption in chivalry by many such metaphors and similes, as well as by his constant, open exaltation of honour. He would have a youth wed honour, not simply woo it. "Perseverance," he says, "keeps honour bright." "Who hates honour hates the gods above."

> *Honour and policy, like unsever'd friends,*
> *I' the war do grow together. Grant that, and tell me*
> *In peace what each of them by the other lose,*
> *That they combine not there.*

IV

SHAKESPEARE portrays numerous knightly characters in his historical plays. Of these none is more valorous than "English John Talbot," "renowned noble gentleman,"—chief hero of the fifteenth-century wars with France. "Above human thought [Talbot] enacted wonders with his sword and lance;" his opponents declared that he was "the devil in arms;" yet he was "the life, the joy," of his friends, and he did his duty to his sovereign with "submissive loyalty of heart." Once, fiercely indignant against a coward captain who had deserted him in danger, he tore the insignia of the Garter from the recreant's knee, declaring that "this ornament of knighthood" was not fit for the infamous. Shakespeare knew various persons to whom he might have pointedly addressed the following pregnant words:

> *When first this order was ordain'd, my lords,*
> *Knights of the Garter were of noble birth,*
> *Valiant and virtuous, full of haughty courage,*
> *Such as were grown to credit by the wars;*
> *Not fearing death, nor shrinking from distress,*

But always resolute in most extremes.
He then that is not furnish'd in this sort
Doth but usurp the sacred name of knight,
Profaning this most honourable order;
And should, if I were worthy to be judge,
Be quite degraded, like a hedge-born swain
That doth presume to boast of gentle blood.

The scenes between Talbot and his son in their last
hours are unforgetable by any one whose heart leaps
up at bravery. The old general sends for the young
man to give him his final instructions, and to bid
him make his escape while there is still time; but he
stoutly refuses to go.

Is my name Talbot? and am I your son?
And shall I fly?

Again the father pleads; still again the son denies.
There is but one possible issue; they go into the battle
together, shouting "St. George and Victory!" Afterwards, when his brave boy has shown by his valour
that he is "sealed the son of chivalry," the old warrior
once more urges him to flee. He pleads a mother's
hopes, their household's name, "my death's revenge,
thy youth, and England's fame," but all to no avail.
Young John refuses to "save a paltry life and slay
bright fame." He will not be "shame's scorn." The
two continue the fight by each other's side. Young
John defends his father with o'ermounting spirit,
and while so doing meets his death. Yet, like Launcelot (like Elaine and Imogen also), as he lay he smiled.

The father dies soon after, with his boy in his arms. Friend and foe pay them deep reverence. They are given burial "as beseemed their worth." "How would it have joyed brave Talbot," wrote Nash in 1592, "to think that after he had lain two hundred years in his tomb, he should triumph again on the stage, and have his bones new embalmed with the tears of ten thousand spectators at least (at several times), who, in the tragedian who represents his person, imagine they behold him fresh bleeding."

Associated with the Talbots was another most notable hero, the Duke of Bedford. His companions spoke of him much as Hector did of Launcelot after death:

> *A braver soldier never couched lance,*
> *A gentler heart did never sway in court.*

Shakespeare likewise admired Duke Humphrey of Gloucester. He did always "bear him like a noble gentleman," good Duke Humphrey, whom the common people loved. When repudiating the accusations of his enemies, he explained:

> *Pity was all the fault that was in me;*
> *For I should melt at an offender's tears,*
> *And lowly words were ransom for his fault.*

He had a "gentle heart" of Chaucer's kind. The king defended him as "virtuous, mild, and too well given to dream on evil;" in his face he saw "the map of honour, truth and loyalty."

King Lear exhibits characters of similar nobility, especially "true-hearted Kent," who could not flatter, and pure Edgar, "whose nature is so far from doing harm that he suspects none." Albany, too, was finely sensitive to honour, and revolted at his wife's cruelty. "Where I could not be honest," he asserted, "I never yet was valiant." It was the tiger Goneril who talked of "milky gentleness" and "harmful mildness;" it was the monster Edmund who declared: "To be tender-minded does not become a sword." Albany remarked with truth:

> *Wisdom and goodness to the vile seem vile;*
> *Filths savour but themselves.*

Chaucer's knight, as we have seen, fought in many places "for our faith." Malory, in almost the closing paragraph of his book, relates that the four warlike knights of King Arthur who remained after the great catastrophe which overwhelmed their fellowship, "went into the Holy Land, there as Jesu Christ was quick and dead. . . . And did many battles upon the miscreants or Turks. And there they died upon a Good Friday for God's sake." But neither Chaucer nor Malory, not to mention Spenser, brings the Crusades so often or so vividly before us as Shakespeare. The poet was enthusiastic for Richard I, whom, despite his arrogance and ferocity, because of his surpassing courage and brilliant personality, men much admire still:

> *Richard, that robbed the lion of his heart*
> *And fought the holy wars in Palestine.*

John of Gaunt, in his famous praise of England, "this dear, dear land," "this precious stone set in the silver sea," glories in it as the "teeming womb of royal kings,"

> *Renowned for their deeds as far from home,*
> *For Christian service and true chivalry,*
> *As is the sepulchre in stubborn Jewry,*
> *Of the world's ransom, blessed Mary's Son.*

"Many a time," said the Bishop of Carlisle, with emotion:

> *Many a time hath banish'd Norfolk fought*
> *For Jesu Christ in glorious Christian field,*
> *Streaming the ensign of the Christian cross*
> *Against black pagans, Turks and Saracens;*
> *And, toil'd with works of war, retir'd himself*
> *To Italy; and there at Venice gave*
> *His body to that pleasant country's earth,*
> *And his pure soul unto his captain Christ,*
> *Under whose colours he had fought so long.*

Constantinople fell almost a century before Shakespeare's birth, and crusading enterprise had wholly ceased; but the spirit of the old encounters the poet sympathetically revived. He showed no contempt for any ideals of the past that led to heroic acts.

V

THE plays of *Henry IV* deserve separate discussion, particularly because of the contrast which Shakespeare there draws between two youths of noble lineage, one of whom was "the theme of honour's tongue," an "all-praised knight," nevertheless a prey to grievous faults, and the other, though stained at first by "riot and dishonour," at the end the paragon's conqueror and the nation's pride—Henry Percy of Northumberland, surnamed Hotspur, and Prince Hal, afterwards King Henry V.

Hotspur is pictured by Shakespeare (varying from authority) as a gallant young knight, who by his high deeds had won "never-dying honour" in all Christendom. The great Douglas addressed him as the "king of honour," and his wife looked on him as a "miracle of men."

> [*His honour*] *stuck upon him as the sun*
> *In the grey vault of heaven, and by his light*
> *Did all the chivalry of England move*
> *To do brave acts. He was indeed the glass*
> *Wherein the noble youth did dress themselves.*

But Shakespeare conceived Hotspur also as madheaded, harebrained, altogether governed by humours, tossed with spleen, easily made drunk with choler, ever ready to "plume himself and bristle up the crest of youth" against supposed indignities, given to flat denials, good mouth-filling oaths, boast, and scorn. "Hot Lord Percy" was prone to call those who angered him contemptuous names—shallow, cowardly, frosty-spirited, lack-brain, dish of skim-milk—and he drew rebuke to himself from many, besides his wife, whose counsel he would not heed. "What think you," asked the irritated king, "of this young Percy's pride?" His father admitted that "imagination of some great exploit [drove] him beyond the bounds of patience." "Fie, Cousin Percy," exclaimed Mortimer, because of the youth's disdainful treatment of Glendower, when he did "cross his humour;" and he is "school'd" by the Earl of Worcester in the following impressive words:

In faith, my lord, you are too wilful-blame:
And since your coming hither have done enough
To put him quite beside his patience.
You must needs learn, lord, to amend this fault.
Though sometimes it shows greatness, courage, blood,—
And that's the dearest grace it renders you,—
Yet oftentimes it doth present harsh rage,
Defect of manners, want of government,
Pride, haughtiness, opinion and disdain;
The least of which haunting a nobleman
Loseth men's hearts and leaves behind a stain
Upon the beauty of all parts besides,
Beguiling them of commendation.

The prominent but strange combination, "wilful-blame," in this extract, has much puzzled the grammarians. One wonders if it may not have been suggested to Shakespeare by the passage in the *Faery*

Queen where Sir Artegall is said to have been left to the will of Radigund "by his own wilful blame." The last books of Spenser's poem appeared a year earlier than *Henry IV*, and the parts concerning Radigund, "a miracle of nature's goodly grace," and false Duessa, both of whom were identified with Mary, Queen of Scots, had caused a national sensation, King James having openly protested against them. It is especially interesting to see that Duessa's mate, bold Blandamour, whom Spenser describes as a "hotspur youth, scorning to be crossed," has features curiously like Shakespeare's northern youth. Blandamour was

> *a jolly youthful knight*
> *That bore great sway in arms and chivalry,*
> *And was indeed a man of mickle might.*

He had, however, a "countenance stern and full of wrath;" he was "too boastful," and used terms of "foul despight;" he accused his companions of being dumpish and sluggish; he was marked by haughty disdain; counsel was lost on him. Once Paridell, his comrade, said:

> *Sir, him wise I never hold*
> *That, having once escaped peril near,*
> *Would afterwards afresh the sleeping evil rear.*

But Blandamour scornfully rejected his advice, and "forth he fiercely pricked that one him scarce could see," only to lose—an example of folly! "Young Hotspur's case at Shrewsbury" is thus explained:

[He] lin'd himself with hope,
Eating the air on promise of supply,
Flatt'ring himself in project of a power
Much smaller than the smallest of his thoughts;
And so, with great imagination
Proper to madmen, led his powers to death,
And winking leap'd into destruction.

Blandamour's motto was: "Fortune friends the bold;" and Hotspur's: *Esperance*—"Die all, die merrily." "I will ease my heart," he said, "although it be with hazard of my head." Hotspur Blandamour and Percy Hotspur have so great likeness that it is difficult to believe it wholly accidental. But be that as it may, we should not fail to observe that both poets strongly deprecate the same faults in knights, while they eagerly applaud in them the same virtues. We recall in this connection Spenser's admirable Sir Calidore, whose "gracious speech did steal men's hearts away," together with his opponent Crudor, a warrior marked by "high disdain, and proud despight of his self-pleasing mind." Calidore, though provoked mightily by the taunts of Crudor's haughty mistress, "did himself from frail impatience refrain," and, when he had overcome his foe, gave him this advice:

Put away proud look and usage stern,
The which shall not to you but foul dishonour yearn.
For nothing is more blameful to a knight,
That court'sy doth as well as arms profess,
However strong and fortunate in fight,
Than the reproach of pride and cruelness.

Meliboe told Calidore that "great ones"

> *oft through pride do their own peril weave,*
> *And through ambition down themselves do drive.*

Hotspur had "ill-weav'd ambition."

Hotspur is to us an exceedingly attractive character because of his idealistic devotion to honour. Prince Hal said the best of him (and it is much) in these words:

> *I do not think a braver gentleman,*
> *More active-valiant or more valiant-young,*
> *More daring or more bold, is now alive*
> *To grace this latter age with noble deeds.*

We all applaud his last appeal to his companions:

> *O gentlemen! the time of life is short;*
> *To spend that shortness basely were too long.*

But to picture Hotspur as a pattern was not Shakespeare's intent. The hero had too many "blameful" attributes—like pride, haughtiness, quick wrath, and self-pleasure; he was ever disposed to folly.

Hotspur's temper, it is explained, had "the excuse of youth and heat of blood." The same excuse may be offered in general for the excesses of chivalry, which, being planned as an ideal for warriors with youth and heat of blood, was bound to be disturbed in manifestation by the defects which usually accompany the qualities of the active-valiant and valiant-young. Because it was peculiarly needed in days of deeds, to counterbalance courage, mediaeval poets laid great stress on "measure." Treatises on chivalry persistently rebuke impatience and disdain, boast and hasty speech, as inconsistent with the pure ideal they held aloft. Chaucer said of his perfect Knight: "Though that he was worthy, he was wise;" and Shakespeare made Lord Bardolph counsel Hotspur's father: "Sweet Earl, divorce not wisdom from your honour."

Hotspur seems characteristically English when he betrays contempt for an effeminate, popinjay lord, "neat and trimly dressed," "perfumed like a milliner," who questioned him with many "holiday and lady terms" when a battle had hardly ceased.

He made me mad
To see him shine so brisk and smell so sweet
And talk so like a waiting gentlewoman
Of guns and drums and wounds, — God save the mark!

Hotspur cared not for "candy courtesy," or "mincing poetry." "I profess not talking," he declared; "I have not well the gift of tongue." In these respects he resembles that other blunt Englishman, the bastard Philip Faulconbridge, natural son of Richard Cœur de Lyon, who, though a "babbler" himself, felt "bethump'd with words" when Hubert de Burgh opened his "large mouth." This "lusty gentleman" was proud of "our lusty English," and had plenty of their independent vigour and strong fidelity to king and land; but he too was blotted with intolerance and self-love.

Prince Hal, in contrast to Hotspur, began his career most ill. His father accused him of "inordinate and low desires," of indulgence in "barren pleasures, rude society," which should not have accompanied the greatness of his blood; he was "almost an alien to the hearts of all at court," a "libertine." Yet, after he had come to recognize that he had been a "truant to chivalry," he turned from his reckless comrades, and proved himself a just and dignified leader, strong in self-control. Prince Hal had always charm. Like Chaucer's Squire, he was "as full of spirit as is the month of May," and able to "witch the world with noble horsemanship." He had "a tear for pity, and a hand open as day for melting charity." When he slew Hotspur in combat, he showed his body courtesy, and revealed his own worthiness in his adieu: "Fare thee well, great heart!" It was not thus that Achilles treated Hector! Prince Hal's last act in the encounter at Shrewsbury was also one of "high courtesy;" he delivered up the great Douglas ransomless and free, saying nobly:

> *His valour shown upon our crests to-day*
> *Hath taught us how to cherish such high deeds,*
> *Even in the bosom of our adversaries.*

Here seems born again the Black Prince, as courteous as brave, whom the poet was soon after to picture in glory at Crécy, with "his most mighty father" standing smiling by, leaving him alone—to win!

When Shakespeare was writing *Henry IV*, he absorbed all he could of the spirit of chivalry as revealed in books on the theme. One of those (not hitherto noted) which he appears to have read is the famous *Law of Arms*, by Chaucer's contemporary, Honoré Bonet. This work, readily accessible to him in English as well as French, concludes with a short section on "What good properties and conditions should be in a king," several features of which (as will be seen in a note*) the poet emphasizes in prominent passages of *Henry IV* and the *Merchant of Venice*. Here we shall examine only a few statements concerning such qualities as Hotspur lacked: "A prince or a lord that cannot put measure in his largess . . . and in all his other deeds of virtue, he is counted not wise." "He should be temperate in his word, that no unfitting word part from his mouth, and be measured that he think always before he speak, with good deliberation. . . . A king's word should be firm." "A prince should be well-measured in his breath, and not be soon moved to ire." Shakespeare makes Troilus illustrate these very precepts. This "true knight," he tells us, was "firm of word," "not soon provok'd"—

Speaking in deeds, and deedless in his tongue. . . .
Yet gives he not till judgement guide his bounty,
Nor dignifies an impure thought with breath.

Spenser represents Sir Calidore as loth to break "the law of arms," and he exhibits the same good qualities. Bonet's remark, "It is not to presume that a king should well govern others that cannot govern his own person," reminds one of what Sir Calidore says in the *Faery Queen*:

> *In vain he seeketh others to suppress,*
> *Who hath not learned himself first to subdue.*

It almost seems like the text of Shakespeare's teaching in *Henry IV*.

VI

THE *Order of Chivalry*, already mentioned more than once, was regularly associated, even bound up, with the *Law of Arms*. It was the most obvious book from which Shakespeare might derive knowledge of the principles which should appropriately inspire his plays on mediaeval heroes. According to the *Order*, "virtue and measure abide in the middle of two extremities, pride and vice." Even as Shakespeare embodied the former of these extremities in Hotspur, so he did the latter in Falstaff. Sir John is perennially fascinating because of his brilliant wit and unquenchable jollity; but we should not fail to note that the poet makes him nearly everything which chivalric moralists reprimanded in a knight. In Caxton's rough rendering of the *Order* is written: "Because a knight being without harness, and that hath no riches for to make his dispences, if he be made knight, him should peradventure hap for need to be a robber, a thief, traitor, liar or beguiler, or have some other vices which be contrary to chivalry—a man lame, or over great, or *over fat*, or that hath any other evil disposition in his body, is not sufficient to be a knight." "The fat knight" Falstaff alone illustrated nearly every vice set forth here, as well as elsewhere, in the *Order*. His over-fatness was, of course, his most prominent characteristic. "An I had but a belly of any indifferency," he lamented, "I were simply the most active fellow in Europe." But thereto he was "heinously unprovided;" he had "an incurable disease of the purse." Prince Hal finally gave him a competency, "that lack of means enforce [him] not to evil."

Falstaff comes on the scene as a robber and thief, and he speedily reveals himself a liar, swaggerer, roisterer, glutton, and "misleader of youth." He is slothful, dishonest, perjured, foul-mouthed, gross— unscrupulous in his relations with the poor Hostess, mean to Shallow, deserving imprisonment (so the Chief Justice thought) as a knave and a rogue —"Wherein worthy, but in nothing?" It shows a strange misunderstanding of Shakespeare's purpose in picturing Falstaff in this light, to have critics worry because Prince Hal, when he became king, banished from court this "tutor and feeder of [his] riots," until such time as he should reform. The *Order* expressly directs: "When any noble prince or high baron hath in his court or in his company, wicked knights, false and traitors, that never finish to admonish him that he do wickedness, . . . much great strength of courage and great noblesse hath such a lord in himself, and greatly is he the friend of chivalry, when he taketh vengeance of such enemies that would take from him and pluck away the weal and honour of chivalry, and corrupt his noble courage." Henry IV feared that his son was degenerate; but Prince Hal (like the poet himself) early redeemed his youthful mistakes. Falstaff, however, having been persistent in evil-doing until old age, was quite beyond cure, and came to a lamentable end. "Every officer, spiritual and temporal," we find in the fifteenth-century *Book of Noblesse*, "should put him in his devoir to the advancing of the common profit;" "voluptuous delights led by sensuality be contrary to the exercising and haunting of arms." The "authority" of this work was an actual Sir John Fastolf. Shakespeare's Sir John was certainly not this man, any more than Oldcastle, the martyr.

Externally Falstaff has the same character as Parolles in *All 's Well*, "a very tainted fellow and full of wickedness," who corrupted by his inducement the " well-derived nature" of Bertram, Count of Rousillon. Parolles was "more saucy with lords and

honourable personages that the commission of [his]
birth and virtue [gave him] heraldry"—"a most notable coward, an infinite and endless liar, an hourly
promise-breaker, the owner of no one good quality
worthy [Bertram's] entertainment." Like Thersites,
he was a loud braggart, yet given to "base fear;" his
tongue alone was too foolhardy; he went backward
when he fought; he was a fox. Parolles and Falstaff
(in a measure) are of the same breed as Malory's
King Mark, also a fox, and a "destroyer of good
knights." When cowardly Mark encountered Launcelot he "made no defence, but tumbled down out of
his saddle to the earth as a sack, and there he lay and
cried Sir Launcelot mercy." But—O that but! how
glad a passage 'tis! Shakespeare endowed Falstaff
with an instinct for good fellowship, so that we are
"bewitched with the rogue's company;" his escapades
are "laughter for a month and a good jest forever."

Falstaff's associate, Master Shallow, took the part
of "Sir Dagonet in Arthur's show," a company of
citizen-archers. This Sir Dagonet, the king's fool,
is described in the *Morte d'Arthur* as "the best
fellow and the merriest in the world;" he made all
his fellows laugh like mad when he chased Mark (on
whom the other knights had played a trick) "through
thick and thin" in a forest. "Arthur loved him passing well, and made him knight with his own hands.
And at every tournament he began to make King

Arthur to laugh." Shakespeare, who exalted fools to such prominence in his plays, must have been strongly drawn to this fun-evoking personage, but probably still more to Sir Dagonet's comrade, Sir Dinadan, another mocker of Mark, the only developed comic character in Malory, whom the poet perhaps remembered in fashioning his own single merry knight. "Send ye for him, my lady Isoud," said Tristram, after telling the queen of Dinadan's exploits, "and I will not be seen, and ye shall hear *the merriest knight that ever ye spake withal* and the maddest talker, and I pray you heartily that ye make him good cheer." As soon as Dinadan arrived, he began to rail against love. "Madam," said Dinadan, "I marvel of Sir Tristram and more other lovers, what aileth them to be so mad and so sotted upon women. Why, said La Belle Isoud, an ye be a knight and be no lover? It is a shame to you. Wherefore ye may not be called a good knight but if ye make quarrel for a lady. Nay, said Sir Dinadan, for the joy of love is too short, and the sorrow thereof, and what cometh thereof, dureth over long. . . . Now, I pray you, said La Belle Isoud, tell me, will ye fight for my love with three knights that have done me great wrong? And in so much as ye be a knight of King Arthur's I require you to do battle for me. Then Sir Dinadan said, I shall say you be as fair a lady as ever I saw any, and much fairer than is my Queen Guinevere, but wit ye well at one word : I will not fight for you with three knights, Heaven defend me. Then Isoud laughed and had good game at him." On another occasion Dinadan boasted of his wisdom in refusing to joust with a knight whom he could not beat; he did not see any point in fighting every errant warrior he met, just for fun.

Falstaff, though not in the least noble like Dinadan, shares his peculiar attitude of common-sense with regard to chivalric hazards; he too thought that the better part of valour was discretion. Falstaff's famous soliloquy on honour before the conflict at Shrewsbury is in Dinadan's humorous vein. "Honour pricks me on. Yea, but how if honour prick me off when I come on? How then? Can honour set to a leg? No. Or an arm? No. Or take away the grief of a wound? No. Honour hath no skill in surgery, then? No. What is honour? A word. What is that word honour? Air; a trim reckoning! . . . I'll none of it. Honour is a mere scutcheon." Falstaff liked not "such grinning honour" as Sir Walter Blunt had, lying dead on the field, slain for his monarch's sake.

Queen Elizabeth seems to have got as much amusement out of merry Falstaff as Guinevere and Ysolt out of merry Dinadan; and at her request, we are told, Shakespeare wrote the *Merry Wives of Windsor*, to show Falstaff in love. It is perhaps not out of place to remark here that in Shakespeare's first play, *Love's*

Labour's Lost, the witty Biron declaims against "Dan Cupid, regent of love-rhymes, the anointed sovereign of sighs and groans," with the cheerful cynicism of Dinadan:

> *What! I love! I sue! I seek a wife!*
> *A woman, that is like a German clock,*
> *Still a-repairing, ever out of frame,*
> *And never going right. . . .*
> *And I to sigh for her! to watch for her!*
> *To pray for her! Go to!*

Rosaline explains to the princess:

> *Biron they call him; but* a merrier man,
> *Within the limit of becoming mirth,*
> I never spent an hour's talk withal.
> *His eye begets occasion for his wit,*
> *For every object that the one doth catch*
> *The other turns to a mirth-moving jest.*

Various critics have detected in Biron something of Shakespeare himself. However that may be, we are profoundly indebted to the poet for his creation of Falstaff, who is mirth-moving as no other knight. Humour did not often find a place in the romances of chivalry, doubtless not often enough to suit a man of Shakespeare's type. Like Chaucer, he felt the need of an occasional laugh in the presence of too perfect paragons. Still, Sir John's jests should not blind us, any more than Sir Thopas' absurdities, to either poet's serious object in presenting his comic figure.

Cervantes died in the same year as Shakespeare;

but Don Quixote, the finest of all burlesques of chivalry, is as appealing now as ever. Though we are highly amused by the hero's fantastic acts, we never fail to recognize the purity of the ideal which guided him. Cervantes may unconsciously have given a death-blow to chivalry by his satire of its weakness in this practical world, but he knew that the same world would be far more materialistic and philistine if the ideal which he ridiculed when carried to excess had never arisen. "I am a knight," said Don Quixote; " as such I shall live; as such, please God, I shall die. I walk in the strait and narrow path of errant chivalry, despising riches but not honour. I have avenged injuries; I have redressed wrongs; I have rebuked insolence; I have no thought which is not upright; I desire to do only good to men. Does one who thinks and acts in this spirit deserve to be treated as a fool? I ask this of Your Excellencies." We cannot imagine Falstaff even comprehending Don Quixote's ideal, let alone acting by it. Yet we wonder what he would have been like had he not been able to subscribe himself "John Falstaff, *Knight;" Sir* John with all Europe: he felt that he belonged to a class as catholic and cosmopolitan as Christendom. When he swore "o' mine honour," "as I am a true knight," "as I am a gentleman," he acknowledged what should have been a force in his case, not only for achievement, but also for restraint.

"Lying, vainness, babbling, drunkenness," Viola points out in *Twelfth Night*, are signs of "corruption" in man. The last of these, drunkenness, seems to have been a besetting sin of English gentlemen in Shakespeare's days.* Sir John Falstaff, Sir Toby Belch, Sir Andrew Aguecheek—Shakespeare's degenerate knights—are all drunkards. And yet, strangely enough, the scenes in which they revel are even now the most popular parts of the plays where they appear. This reveals a noteworthy fact. Falstaff lies, to be sure, but he lies so palpably that we do not lay it up against him; if he lied meanly, he would be hissed off the stage. Anyone among us who shows vanity, or babbles effeminately, is despised; but, while we do not approve, we tolerate drunkenness, even in gentlemen. To this day an Englishman may get "drunk as a lord," and be forgiven. On the contrary, if a French or Spanish gentleman were to drink similarly to coarse excess, he would commit an offence that his countrymen would hardly condone. "All Europe," save residents of Teutonic lands, believe with St. Louis: "It is passing foul for a *preud'omme* to get drunk." When gentle Rosalind asserts that certain abominable fellows "betray themselves to every modern censure, worse than drunkards," we may feel sure that we hear Shakespeare's own condemnation of a common vice opposed to chivalry.

Rosalind deprecated "those that are in the extremity of either" melancholy or laughing. The *Order of Chivalry*, we have seen, applauded "virtue and measure," which "abide in the middle of two extremities, pride and vice." Shakespeare portrays Prince Hal in the end ("Let the end try the man"!) without the excesses of either Hotspur or Falstaff, and makes him consciously aspire to virtue and measure. Prince Hal wished to be a worthy king, and as such, following the *Order*, he had to make himself "chivalry incorporate." Shakespeare loved this royal hero; he gave him the highest hopes of knighthood.

VII

In *Hamlet* we find another interesting contrast between two aspirants to honour. Laertes is preëminently a man of action, who, when enraged by his father's murder, immediately stirs up the people to revolt against the king, and demands revenge. He indignantly refuses to act calmly, as the queen suggests. It was not in his nature to stop to reason, and he goes to the extreme of defiance.

> *I dare damnation. To this point I stand,*
> *That both the worlds I give to negligence,*
> *Let come what comes; only I'll be reveng'd*
> *Most throughly for my father.*

When the king acquaints him with the manner of Polonius' death, his first question is why the slayer has not been proceeded against before. He is eager to show himself his father's son "in deeds more than in words." Hamlet praised Laertes as "a very noble youth," and was very sorry he so forgot himself as to address him rudely. He asked Laertes to pardon this wrong "as a gentleman;" but the latter explained that, while his nature was thereby satisfied, his honour could not be so readily appeased. When wounded to death, Laertes avowed shame for having yielded to Claudius' subtle deceptions, declaring that he himself was "justly killed by [his] own treachery."

Hamlet recognized the likeness of his grievance to that of Laertes; "by the image of my cause," he said, "I see the portraiture of his." Nevertheless, he conducted himself in a manner very different from that of his friend; he was afflicted by indecision under circumstances demanding clear purpose and quick action. The ghost of his father must needs appear a second time "to whet [his] almost blunted purpose;" and he thus argues:

> *Sure, He that made us with such large discourse,*
> *Looking before and after, gave us not*
> *That capability and godlike reason*
> *To fust in us unus'd. Now, whether it be*
> *Bestial oblivion, or some craven scruple*
> *Of thinking too precisely on the event —*
> *A thought which, quarter'd, hath but one part wisdom,*
> *And ever three parts coward, — I do not know*
> *Why yet I live to say, "This thing's to do,"*
> *Sith I have cause, and will, and strength and means,*
> *To do't.*

Hamlet here reveals one source of conflict between the spirit of the Middle Ages and that of the Renaissance: the former inclined men to act without meditation, the latter to meditate without action. Even as Shakespeare said to the mediaeval knight: "Divorce not wisdom from your honour," he said to the Renaissance prince:

> *Rightly to be great,*
> *Is not to stir without great argument,*
> *But, greatly to find quarrel in a straw,*
> *When honour's at the stake.*

He makes Hamlet rejoice in the rashness which, contrary to habit, he exhibited on his way to England.

> *Our indiscretion sometimes serves us well,*
> *When our deep plots do pall; and that should teach us,*
> *There's a divinity that shapes our ends,*
> *Rough-hew them how we will.*

Hamlet was endowed with chivalric qualities. The king pronounced him so above being suspicious— "most generous and free from all contrivings"—that he would not examine the foils in the match; Fortinbras had praise for him as a royal soldier; Horatio bade him farewell as a sweet prince with a noble heart; and "the general gender" bore him great love. But Hamlet, as portrayed by Shakespeare, was unlike any mediaeval hero; he was swayed by his mind. Ophelia, dwelling upon her lover's "noble and most sovereign reason," pictured him first as a courtier and afterwards as a scholar.

> *O, what a noble mind is here o'erthrown!*
> *The courtier's, soldier's, scholar's, eye, tongue, sword;*
> *The expectancy and rose of the fair state.*
> *The glass of fashion and the mould of form,*
> *The observ'd of all observers!*

Ophelia found Hamlet keen, and he reveals intellectual subtlety in his every remark. It is he who exclaims: "What a piece of work is a man! How noble in reason! How infinite in faculty;" and into his mouth the poet put the great philosophical inquiry:

> *To be, or not to be: that is the question.*
> *Whether 't is nobler in the mind to suffer*
> *The slings and arrows of outrageous fortune,*
> *Or to take arms against a sea of troubles,*
> *And by opposing end them.*

A Spenserian courtier might easily, but a Chaucerian knight would never, have questioned himself as Hamlet does. Too much meditation, Shakespeare saw, "puzzles the will," and hampers exploits.

> *Conscience does make cowards of us all;*
> *And thus the native hue of resolution*
> *Is sicklied o'er with the pale cast of thought,*
> *And enterprises of great pith and moment,*
> *With this regard, their currents turn awry,*
> *And lose the name of action.*

The poet's chief heroes are men of action rather than of thought, of deeds rather than of words.

Nay, if we talk of reason,
Let's shut our gates, and sleep. Manhood and honour
Should have hare-hearts, would they but fat their thoughts
With this cramm'd reason. Reason and respect
Make livers pale, and lustihood deject.

Hamlet was the "chiefest courtier" of Claudius; but he treats the other courtiers with measured contempt. He pierces the deceits of Rosencrantz and Guildenstern, terms Polonius a "wretched fool," and ridicules the "golden words" of Osric the waterfly: "Sir, here is newly come to court, Laertes; believe me, an absolute gentleman, full of most excellent differences, of very soft society and great showing: indeed, to speak feelingly of him, he is the card or calendar of gentry, for you shall find in him the continent of what part a gentleman would see." The "absolute gentleman," Laertes, was expert in courtly exercises, and widely travelled. He had won the praise of the gem of French horsemen ("and they can well on horseback"), but he was ready to use a poisoned rapier and a poisoned potion to achieve revenge. The practice of poisoning, Shakespeare believed, flourished in crafty, "drug-damn'd" Italy, and was not censured by the Italianate at the English court. Some of his countrymen actually imitated the "false Italian, as poisonous-tongu'd as handed." They admired Machiavel, whom he called "murd'rous." Most of them, however, merely learned foolish atti-

tudes from far travel. "Farewell, monsieur traveller,"
said Rosalind to the mannered Jaques. "Look you
lisp and wear strange suits; disable all the benefits of
your own country; be out of love with your nativity,
and almost chide God for making you that countenance you are; or I will scarce think you have swam
in a gondola." Shakespeare here shows open sympathy with the prejudices of men of the Ascham
type. He had no desire to see a condition in England
when "manhood is melted into courtesies, and men
only turned into tongue, and trim ones too," when
a man is "as valiant as Hercules that only tells a lie
and swears it." Yet he thought one could not be
a perfect man, "not being try'd and tutor'd in the
world," and he approved anyone who was really

complete in feature and in mind
With all good grace to grace a gentleman.

Armado was thought a "complete" man; but his
was a different sort of completeness; he was "most
dainty," "fashion's own knight," a gamester.*

"Truly," says the clown in *All's Well*, "if God
have lent a man any manners, he may easily put it
off at court." Shakespeare found particular objection
to court manners in the flattery which was apt to
mark them. Therefore he makes Hamlet protest to
loyal Horatio:

Nay, do not think I flatter;
For what advancement may I hope from thee,

That no revénue hast but thy good spirits
To feed and clothe thee? Why should the poor be flatter'd?
No, let the candied tongue lick absurd pomp,
And crook the pregnant hinges of the knee,
Where thrift may follow fawning.

Other taints of court conduct are emphasized in *Cymbeline*, where Belarius contrasts his free life with that which men of his class led in nearness to the king:

O, this life
Is nobler than attending for a check,
Richer than doing nothing for a bribe,
Prouder than rustling in unpaid-for silk.
Such gains the cap of him that makes him fine,
Yet keeps his book uncross'd. No life to ours.

When the young princes whom he is fostering in the mountains protest that they are only like the beasts they chased, having no experience, that they are imprisoned and in bondage for lack of opportunity and ignorance, and still show themselves unpersuaded, their guardian resumes:

Did you but know the city's usuries,
And felt them knowingly; the art o' the court,
As hard to leave as keep; whose top to climb
Is certain falling, or so slipp'ry that
The fear's as bad as falling; the toil o' the war,
A pain that only seems to seek out danger
I' the name of fame and honour; which dies i' the search,
And hath as oft a slanderous epitaph
As record of fair act; nay, many times,
Doth ill deserve by doing well; what's worse,
Must curtsy at the censure.

Belarius thereupon illustrates the situation by his own experience, explaining how he was richly rewarded when victorious as a soldier, but, having suffered from the machinations of two villains who swore he was a traitor and "whose false oaths prevail'd before [his] perfect honour," he was unjustly banished. "Uncertain favour"! Yet the event brought him joy; he had lived some twenty years in "honest freedom." Shakespeare might have read similar words in the *Curial* of Alain Chartier, translated by Caxton in 1484, "at the instance and request of a noble and virtuous earl," in which work the author pointed out with emphasis to his rustic brother the miseries of court life, urging him to stay in peace and honesty at home. It is clear, however, that Shakespeare's condemnation of ordinary courtiers was not merely an echo, or a convention; he knew what was happening about him to friends and foes of Elizabeth.

Perhaps he also found in actual life the models of his ideal courtiers. We read of Posthumus that he

> *liv'd in court—*
> *Which rare it is to do—most prais'd, most lov'd,*
> *A sample to the youngest, to the more mature*
> *A glass that feated them, and to the graver*
> *A child that guided dotards.*

This "true knight" seems almost to image Sir Philip Sidney:

> *He is one*
> *The truest manner'd, such a holy witch*

That he enchants societies into him;
Half all men's hearts are his . . .
He sits 'mongst men like a descended god:
He hath a kind of honour sets him off,
More than a mortal seeming.

Posthumus, like Sidney, was avid of learning, and "did incline to sadness, not knowing why;" no other man was endowed with "so fair an outward and such stuff within." He is strongly contrasted to miserable Cloten, a wrathy, profane, boastful, contemptuous "ass," a mean gambler and lustful wooer, together with various other "that-way-accomplished courtiers" of Britain and Italy who appear in the play. We think also of Lord Herbert of Cherbury, well-reputed "both for learning and courage," who in youth avoided courtly companions because he observed in them "much ill-example and debauchery." "Public duty," he wrote, "did not hinder me yet to follow my beloved studies in a country life for the most part; although sometimes also I resorted to court, without yet that I had any ambition there and much less was tainted with those corrupt delights incident to the times."

As had often been done by writers before him, Shakespeare portrayed a noble courtier of the past as a model for his own day. The King of France describes Bertram's father as possessed of wit without scorn, as a man of honour without levity.

> *Contempt nor bitterness*
> *Were in his pride or sharpness; if they were,*
> *His equal had awak'd them, and his honour,*
> *Clock to itself, knew the true minute when*
> *Exception bid him speak, and at this time*
> *His tongue obey'd his hand. Who were below him*
> *He us'd as creatures of another place,*
> *And bow'd his eminent top to their low ranks,*
> *Making them proud of his humility,*
> *In their poor praise he humbled. Such a man*
> *Might be a copy to these younger times;*
> *Which, followed well, would demonstrate them now*
> *But goers backward.*

The corollary of dissatisfaction with the court was enthusiasm for the country. "Gods, what lies I have heard," exclaimed Imogen at Belarius' retreat:

> *Our courtiers say all's savage but at court.*
> *Experience, O, thou disprov'st report!*

Be it because of his own experience or not, Shakespeare betrays a most living sense of that joy in rural life which English gentlemen have so conspicuously shown. Nowhere does this appear more than in *As You Like It*, a delightful comedy, interpenetrated with thoughts of gentleness. There we read of the gentle duke, father of Rosalind, who dwelt in the forest of Arden, "like the old Robin Hood of England," and "a many merry men with him," fleeting the time carelessly "as they did in the golden world." For this play Shakespeare utilized Thomas Lodge's version of the fourteenth-century outlaw tale of *Gamelyn*, which seems to have appealed long before to Chaucer, for it is preserved in manuscripts of the *Canterbury Tales*, and is thought to have been one which he intended to rewrite. Chaucer had a veritable genius for discovering what his countrymen were later to admire, and his taste and Shakespeare's singularly agree. In his *Former Age* (adapted from Boethius), Chaucer also exalted "a blissful life, a peaceable, and a sweet," such as men were imagined to have lived in the happy time when no palace-chambers existed, and everyone kept faith to other. Spenser developed the idea finely in the *Faery Queen*. Old Meliboe, who guarded Pastorella, did not long for "the world's gay shows," but rejoiced in "the simple sort of life that shepherds lead," quiet, free, and fortunate, spending all his nights in "silver sleep," the fields his food, the flock his raiment, envying no one, envied by none.

> [*He*] *set his rest among the rustic sort,*
> *Rather than hunt still after shadows vain*
> *Of courtly favour, fed with light report*
> *Of every blast, and sailing always in the port. . . .*
> *For who had tasted once (as oft did he)*
> *The happy peace which there doth overflow . . .*
> *Would never more delight in* painted show.

Shakespeare, we have sufficient evidence, was acquainted with this passage. It is in the same mood as Meliboe that the gentle duke speaks to his followers:

> *Now, my co-mates, and brothers in exile,*
> *Hath not old custom made this life more sweet*

> *Than that of* painted pomp? *Are not these woods*
> *More free from peril than the envious court?*

In the woods, "exempt from public haunt," was no flattery; there men lived sweetly in quiet. Celia declared, when she accompanied Rosalind from the court, that she went "to liberty and not to banishment."

> *Who doth ambition shun*
> *And loves to live i' the sun,*
> *Seeking the food he eats,*
> *And pleased with what he gets,*
> *Come hither, come hither, come hither.*

The shepherd Corin sums up wisely the whole matter of court *versus* country, when he replies to Touchstone's assertion that if he was never at court, he never saw good manners: "Those that are good manners at the court are as ridiculous in the country as the behaviour in the country is most mockable at court." Unlike Spenser, Shakespeare placed the enlightened country gentleman above the courtier, especially if the latter was Italianate. He gave haughtiness no countenance and accomplishments no superior mien.

At the very opening of *As You Like It*, the poet indicates views regarding the education of noble youth in accord with those of English schoolmasters. Good Sir Rowland de Bois, whom all the world esteemed honourable, and whom the gentle duke loved as his soul, carefully arranged for Orlando's education. Oliver, however, neglected his younger brother, kept him "rustically at home," and bred his horses better, for they were "taught their manage and to that end riders dearly hir'd." Finally Orlando protested: " My father charg'd you in his will to give me good education. You have trained me like a peasant, obscuring and hiding from me all gentleman-like qualities. The spirit of my father grows strong in me, and I will no longer endure it; therefore allow me such exercises as become a gentleman." If Orlando had no such education as humanists demanded, he had the blood in his veins and the example of his father, as guides to excellence; he exhibits a character of chivalric beauty. Even Oliver, in secret, acknowledged Orlando's distinction: "He's gentle, never school'd and yet learned, full of noble device, *of all sorts enchantingly beloved*, and, indeed, so much in the heart of the world, and especially of my own people, who best know him, that I am altogether misprised." Nothing is more striking as a witness to the hero's knightliness than his treatment of the family servant, Adam, whom Oliver spurned as an "old dog." Adam's heart went out to Orlando:

> *My young master! — O, my gentle master!*
> *O, my sweet master! O, you memory*
> *Of old Sir Rowland! . . .*
> *Why are you virtuous? Why do people love you?*
> *And wherefore are you gentle, strong and valiant?*

When he offers the youth all his life's savings, to help him in need, the latter exclaims:

> *O good old man, how well in thee appears*
> *The constant service of the antique world,*
> *When service sweat for duty, not for meed!*
> *Thou art not for the fashion of these times,*
> *Where none will sweat but for promotion,*
> *And having that do choke their service up*
> *Even with the having.*

Adam replies, with the devotion of "pure love:"

> *Master, go on, and I will follow thee*
> *To the last gasp, with truth and loyalty.*

To obtain relief for this faithful friend, Orlando, with drawn sword, breaks into the company of the gentle duke, and defiantly demands food. Whereupon the latter speaks:

> *Art thou thus bolden'd, man, by thy distress:*
> *Or else a rude despiser of good manners,*
> *That in civility thou seem'st so empty? . . .*
> *What would you have? Your gentleness shall force*
> *More than your force move us to gentleness.*

Orlando at once changes his tone:

> *Speak you so gently? Pardon me, I pray you:*
> *I thought that all things had been savage here;*
> *And therefore put I on the countenance*
> *Of stern commandment. But whate'er you are . . .*
> *If ever you have look'd on better days;*
> *If ever been where bells have knoll'd to church;*
> *If ever sat at any good man's feast;*
> *If ever from your eyelids wiped a tear,*

And know what 'tis to pity and be pitied;
Let gentleness my strong enforcement be,
In the which hope, I blush, and hide my sword.

The duke acknowledges himself moved; he has assuredly been knoll'd to church with holy bell, and wiped his eyes of "drops that sacred pity hath engender'd;" he begs Orlando to sit down "in gentleness," and command anything that may minister to his want. A special interest attaches to these scenes, because tradition asserts that Shakespeare himself acted the part of Adam. Shakespeare, as much as Chaucer, would have us understand that gentleness begets gentleness, even perhaps as "the sight of lovers feedeth those in love." He wrote with all his heart in praise of the constant service of the antique world, glorifying truth and loyalty. "Kindness," he makes Oliver say after his conversion, is "nobler ever than revenge."

As You Like It is all surrounded by an atmosphere of graciousness; but it is not only here that "the air nimbly and sweetly recommends itself unto our gentle senses;" similar charm is noticeable in *A Midsummer Night's Dream.* It may be that the poet saw royal revels at Kenilworth and elsewhere, in youth and later, and was therefore the better able to write of the open joys of "gentles," of the abridgements of fair pastime, of the "musical confusion of hounds and echo in conjunction," of feasts held in great solemnity, all touched upon in that brilliant play. But to be able, also, to make his readers feel the sweet courtliness of Theseus and Hippolyta, to voice without any discordant note the moods of gentle lovers in palace-halls, was more than a trick of "strong imagination;" it required knowledge of antique fables, large sympathy with the life of chivalry that they revealed, and, above all, a personal wish for gentleness.

Mediaeval chivalric writers occupied themselves chiefly with the relations of individuals to one another in cosmopolitan fellowship. They exalted wise *self*-government, but scarcely mentioned patriotism or politics. On the other hand, courtiers of the Renaissance strongly urged young men to contribute to the public weal of their various lands. They promoted wise *civic* government as a prime need of civilization. With chivalric temper, Shakespeare shows himself incomparably more interested in problems of personal conduct than in questions of state.

VIII

In one of his finest sonnets, the poet thus ruminates on the love-writings of former days:

> *When in the chronicle of wasted time*
> *I see descriptions of the fairest wights,*
> *And beauty making beautiful old rhyme*
> *In praise of ladies dead, and lovely knights;*

Then, in the blazon of sweet beauty's best
Of hand, of foot, of lip, of eye, of brow,
I see their antique pen would have express'd
Ev'n such a beauty as you master now.
So all their praises are but prophecies
Of this our time, all you prefiguring.

Chivalric love manifestly prefigured that which Shakespeare exalted. There is no very important difference between his views and Chaucer's on this theme: both of them laughed genially at the excesses of courtly "service," but both were sweetly sensitive to honourable true love, and illustrated its effects on idealistic hearts.

When Valentine exclaims in *The Two Gentlemen of Verona:* "O, gentle Proteus, love's a mighty lord!" he is merely quoting from the Knight's Tale:

The god of love, a! benedicite,
How mighty and how greet a lord is he!

Valentine himself has striking similarity to Chaucer's Troilus. He is introduced to us as a noble youth, zealous for honour, but disdainful of love, who takes pleasure in chiding Proteus, a "love-wounded" friend, because of his unhappy plight. We remember how Troilus, if he saw a companion sigh for a lady, "would smile and hold it folly," and speak thus:

"*I have herd told, pardieux, of your livinge,*
Ye lovers, and your lewede observaunces,
And which a labour *folk han in winninge*
Of love, and, in the keping, which doutances;

And whan your preye is lost, wo and penaunces;
O verrey foles! nyce and blinde be ye;
Ther nis not oon can war by other be."

But this scorner of "love's pains" was altered with
a look from Cressida and "waxed suddenly most
subject unto love." He caught a "malady" from
which he felt that he was sure to die.

And fro this forth tho refte him love his sleep
And made his mete his foo; and eek his sorwe
Gan multiplye, that who-so toke keep,
It shewed in his hewe, both eve and morwe.

In like manner, Valentine was suddenly "metamor-
phosed with a mistress," and showed all the "special
marks" of love. Speed, who humorously enumerated
these, declared that not an eye that saw him but was
"a physician to comment on [his] malady." The hero
was humbled and confessed his fault:

I have done penance for contemning love;
Whose high imperious thoughts have punish'd me
With bitter fasts, with penitential groans,
With nightly tears, and daily heart-sore sighs;
For in revenge of my contempt of love,
Love hath chas'd sleep from my enthralled eyes,
And made them watchers of mine own heart's sorrow.

In *Love's Labour's Lost*, which also turns on how
the proud in love may be abased, Biron appears as
another scoffer reproved. After witnessing how the
king, Dumain, and Longaville (who had all vowed

to disregard ladies) privately vented their mournful longings, he exclaims:

> *O, what a scene of foolery have I seen,*
> *Of sighs, of groans, of sorrow, and of teen!*

Yet he himself could not resist the "almighty dreadful little might" of Dan Cupid, and languished for Rosaline, who steadily mocked him for his pains. Biron was born again in witty Benedick, who similarly flouted love. "I do much wonder," he says early in *Much Ado*, "that one man seeing how much another man is a fool when he dedicates his behaviours to love, will, after he hath laughed at such shallow follies in others, become the argument of his own scorn by falling in love." Notwithstanding, he ends by marrying Beatrice, through a trick. "Cupid kills some with arrows, some with traps."

Shakespeare had the sixth book of the *Faery Queen* fresh in memory when he wrote his early plays, and may have recalled then how Sir Calidore "was unawares surpris'd in subtile bands of the blind boy," caught like a bird, and brought suddenly to adore fairest Pastorella. Of this charming maiden (whom the poet was later to revive in Perdita) we read:

> *Many a one*
> *Burned in her love, and with sweet pleasing pain*
> *Full many a night for her did sigh and groan.*

She had not cared a whit for previous suitors, but she

quickly yielded herself to the courteous stranger, as Silvia did to Valentyne. One wonders if Spenser's words regarding her, "Ne was there shepherd's swain but her did honour," did not find an echo in the following song:

> *Who is Silvia? What is she,*
> *That all our swains commend her?*
> *Holy, fair, and wise is she;*
> *The heaven such grace did lend her,*
> *That she might admired be.*
>
> *Is she kind as she is fair?*
> *For beauty lives with kindness;*
> *Love doth to her eyes repair*
> *To help him of his blindness,*
> *And, being help'd, inhabits there.*

Troilus felt the "plesaunce of love" which is "in gentle hearts aye ready to repair." He discovered that "love had his dwelling within the subtle streams of [Cressida's] eyes," and he addressed the god "with piteous voice:"

> *Ye stonden in hire eyen mightily,*
> *As in a place unto your vertu digne.*

Shakespeare often emphasizes the wonder in a mortal eye, but nowhere more strongly than in Biron's brilliant speech, where he affirms that love is "first learned in a lady's eyes" and "lives not alone immured in the brain."

> *From women's eyes this doctrine I derive:*
> *They sparkle still the right Promethean fire;*

They are the books, the arts, the academes,
That show, contain, and nourish all the world,
Else none at all in aught proves excellent.

Fancy, the poet elsewhere says, is bred not in the head but in the heart.

It is engender'd in the eyes,
With gazing fed.

Love's Labour's Lost has various Chaucerian touches. Dumain, for example, sings of "love, whose month is ever May;" and Longaville tries to justify breaking his oath by representing his lady as a goddess, not a woman, his love not of earth but of heaven. Most noteworthy, however, is the fact that, like Chaucer, the poet here reveals a disposition to smile at conventional love, as well as at the "painted rhetoric" which was used to proclaim it. Chaucer tells us of the crying and the woe of Palamon after he has been "hurt through [his] eye into [his] heart" by a glance at Emelye, and of his "youling and clamour" after Arcite has been let out of prison; he describes repeatedly the affliction of devotees of Cupid, and makes Theseus ask mockingly (in the passage where the god of love is spoken of as a mighty lord):

Who may been a fool, but-if he love? . . .
And yet they wenen for to been ful wyse
That serven love, for aught that may bifalle!

Shakespeare speaks likewise in his own *Troilus:*

For to be wise and love
Exceeds man's might; that dwells with gods above,

which strongly resembles Spenser's form of the old
idea:

To be wise and eke to love
Is granted scarce to gods above.

Lord Bacon made a similar remark in his essay on
Love: "It was well said that it is impossible to love
and be wise;" but he quoted the adage from the
Latin. Bacon, one may say in passing, could no more
have written Shakespeare's poems of love than Lord
Chesterfield could have written the songs of Burns.
In striking contrast to Shakespeare, Bacon shows
little feeling for chivalry anywhere in his works.

The vows of the lovers who lost their labour, Biron
called "flat treason 'gainst the kingly state of youth."
As by Chaucer, so by Shakespeare, love is pictured
as the chief idealistic impulse of the noble young.
The countess says in *All's Well* (which was probably earlier called *Love's Labour's Won*):

It is the show and seal of nature's truth,
Where love's strong passion is impress'd in youth.

The clown sings in *Twelfth Night*:

What is love? 't is not hereafter.
Present mirth hath present laughter;
    What 's to come is still unsure.
In delay there lies no plenty;
Then come kiss me, Sweet-and-twenty,
    Youth 's a stuff will not endure.

Valentine, a mirror of chivalry, has his foil in Proteus, who protests all truth and faith, but turns out to be a "subtle, perjured, false, disloyal man," of the light o' love sort that Chaucer particularly abhorred. "Thou hast deceived so many with thy vows," Silvia says to him, indicating how often he was forsworn. Proteus asks: "In love, who respects friend?" and Silvia answers: "All men but Proteus." She advises him to devote himself whole-heartedly to his "first best love," and not have "plural faith." If he were really a true lover, he would sepulchre his love in his lady's grave. Proteus was as vile as Jason (who acted "with feigning and every subtle deed") and all the other villains of the *Legend of Good Women*, which poem Shakespeare knew well. He was even ready to take Silvia at a disadvantage, and love her "'gainst the nature of love," that is "force" her. Valentine denounced his treachery, but generously (too generously for probability!) accepted his repentance; whereupon Proteus bewailed his vice in words that Chaucer might have used:

O heaven! were man
But constant, he were perfect. That one error
Fills him with faults; makes him run through all the sins.

How often the earlier poet had emphasized this thought:

We men may say more, swear more; but, indeed,

> *Our shows are more than will; for still we prove*
> *Much in our vows, but little in our love!*

In Thurio, moreover, we see a despicable lover, of
Chaucer's "dung-hill" kind. The duke rightly (from
the point of view of chivalry) calls him "degenerate
and base" when he abandons Silvia with the words:

> *I hold him but a fool that will endanger*
> *His body for a girl that loves him not.*

Shakespeare's own view was this:

> *Love is not love*
> *Which alters when it alteration finds,*
> *Or bends with the remover to remove.*
> *O, no! it is an ever-fixèd mark*
> *That looks on tempests and is never shaken;*
> *It is the star to every wand'ring bark,*
> *Whose worth's unknown, although his height be taken.*
> *Love's not Time's fool, though rosy lips and cheeks*
> *Within his bending sickle's compass come.*
> *Love alters not with the brief hours and weeks,*
> *But bears it out even to the edge of doom.*

Other chivalric sentiments occur in *The Two Gentlemen of Verona:* "they love least that let men know
their love;" "truth hath better deeds than words
to grace it;" "hope is a lover's staff;" "lovers break
not hours;" and "scorn at first makes after-love
the more." "We are betroth'd," said Valentine. "I
am betroth'd," said Silvia. As genuine lovers of the
mediaeval type, they were prepared to die rather than
violate their plighted word.

Cressida "loved Troilus right for the first sight," and Chaucer approved her "sudden love." Marlowe shared his feelings, and Shakespeare too. In *As You Like It*, the latter wrote:

> *Dead shepherd! Now I find thy saw of night*
> *Who ever loved, that loved not at first sight.*

> *It was a lover and his lass,*
>   *With a hey, and a ho, and a hey nonino,*
> *That o'er the green cornfield did pass*
>   *In the spring time, the only pretty ring time,*
> *When birds do sing, hey ding a ding, ding;*
> *Sweet lovers love the spring.*

"The poor world," said Rosalind humorously, "is almost six thousand years old, and in all this time there was not any man died in his own person, *videlicet*, in a love cause. Troilus had his brains dashed out with a Grecian club; yet he did what he could to die before; and he is one of the patterns of love." The faithful shepherd Silvius told her "what 't is to love," after the pattern of such a knight:

> *It is to be all made of sighs and tears . . .*
> *It is to be all made of faith and service . . .*
> *It is to be all made of fantasy;*
> *All made of passion, and all made of wishes;*
> *All adoration, duty, and observance,*
> *All humbleness, all patience, and impatience,*
> *All purity, all trial, all observance.*

Rosalind had heard "many lectures" against love from "an old religious uncle," who had taxed her whole sex with "many giddy offences." Had she been willing to disclose them, we should have found that they resembled those which Chaucer learned from mediaeval clerks, and which Cressida might have acquired from her old irreligious uncle, Pandar. Rosalind, all the while deeply enamoured of Orlando, is merely playful in her mockery. She voices the sentiments of both Chaucer and Shakespeare in her counsel to Phebe: "Foul is most foul, being foul to be a scoffer." If one really scorns love, one must be, like Beatrice, "self-endeared;" one must have self-love, "which is the most inhibited sin in the canon." True love and self-love have ever been yoked together unequally.

In *A Midsummer-Night's Dream* we find Cupid again supreme, with a plenty of love's vows, entreaties, and languishings, among gentles—"love-in-idleness." The play illustrates Lysander's view:

> *Ah me! for aught that ever I could read,*
> *Could ever hear by tale or history,*
> *The course of true love never did run smooth.*

Hermia's soul consented not to give sovereignty to Demetrius, but she idolized Lysander, lord of "true gentleness." Under delusion, the latter strove "to honour Helen, and to be her knight," but when himself, he was a faithful follower of his betrothed lady. "Thy love n'er alter, till thy sweet life end!" she said to him. And he replied:

Amen, Amen, to that fair prayer say I;
And then end life, when I end loyalty.

Her companion, Helena, with a "gentle tongue" and
a heart "as true as steel," was drawn as irresistibly to
Demetrius as the Nut Brown Maid to her lover, and
was ready to suffer any spurns or strokes to follow
him. Gentle Puck called him a churl when he seemed
to be a "lack-love." Shakespeare put as much contempt as Chaucer into the word "churl."

Another Helena, in *All's Well*, reminds one of
Malory's Elaine. The countess dwelt on her "pure
love," and her one desire was to "wish chastely and
love dearly."

I know I love in vain, strive against hope;
Yet in this captious and intenible sieve
I still pour in the waters of my love,
And lack not to lose still.

Helena was ready to live as the "servant" of her dear
lord and master, Bertram, and to die his "vassal."
This chivalric attitude of willing service on the part
of one who, having won sovereignty, was delighted
to give it back, is found frequently in Shakespeare's
heroines, as, for example, in Portia, who speaks thus
of herself to Bassanio:

Happiest of all is that her gentle spirit
Commits itself to yours to be directed,
As from her lord, her governor, her king.

Miranda says to Ferdinand: "I'll be your servant

whether you will or no;" but he replies: "My mistress, dearest, and I thus humble ever." Ferdinand was a true lover, who loved at first sight. "Love sought is good, but, given unsought, is better."

We have already seen that Shakespeare's earliest published poems concerned love. There is a strong Ovidian atmosphere about *Venus and Adonis*, which is paralleled in some of Chaucer's works: but Shakespeare felt as keenly as Chaucer, or even Malory, the difference between love and lust.

> *Love comforteth like sunshine after rain,*
> *But lust's effect is tempest after sun;*
> *Love's gentle spring doth always fresh remain,*
> *Lust's winter comes ere summer half be done;*
> *Love surfeits not, lust like a glutton dies;*
> *Love is all truth, lust full of forged lies.*

For some reason best known to himself, Shakespeare, shortly after he had written *As You Like It*, chose to represent Cressida as a sheer wanton. Rosalind resembles Chaucer's heroine more at the start.

> *The people praise her for her virtues.*

> *Her very silence and her patience*
> *Speak to the people, and they pity her.*

She, too, awakes instant love in a valiant chivalric youth; she, too, has both physical charm and quick intelligence; she is feminine as well as shrewd. Rosalind, however, cannot understand any one being "not true in love." In her affection for Orlando was "matter from the heart," not as in the new Cressida's—"words, words, mere words." The mediaeval Cleopatra is no more like Shakespeare's than the first Cressida resembles the second. Chaucer emphasized the ruth of his woeful heroine when her knight was slain. She had sworn to be all freely his, and made a covenant with herself, so far as it was "unreprovable" with her womanhood, to feel as he felt, come life or death. She sought her own end "with good cheer"—"Was never unto her love a truer queen." Here is nothing of Shakespeare's "amorous surfeiter," "the serpent of old Nile," who compassed the shame of Antony.

According to Shakespeare, Antony's honour died because of his lady's charms. He was "beguil'd to the very heart of loss." This situation is frequently paralleled in mediaeval romance. Chrétien de Troies, for example, represents Yvain, Knight of the Lion, one of the most valiant heroes of the Round Table, as succumbing to the witchery of a *fée*, Lunette, who kept him long from prowess; and Guinglain, the Fair Unknown, had to be lured from his fairy mistress of the Golden Isle by special appeals to his honour. At Arthur's request, he married the devoted Esmerée, but he continued to long for his *dame d'amour*, no angel of heaven, but a "most sovereign creature" of the Otherworld.

Age cannot wither her, nor custom stale
Her infinite variety.

In an interesting scene of *King John*, two ladies
present honour from different points of view. Blanche
of Castile, who has just married the Dauphin, tries to
keep him from taking up arms against the English,
saying:

> *Now shall I see thy love. What motive may*
> *Be stronger with thee than the name of wife?*

To which Constance, Prince Arthur's mother, makes
direct reply:

> *That which upholdeth him that thee upholds,*
> *His honour. O thine honour, Lewis, thine honour!*

Honour *versus* love! We remember what Lovelace
wrote:

> *I could not love thee, Dear, so much,*
> *Loved I not Honour more.*

Celia says to Rosalind: "By mine honour I will; and
when I break that oath let me turn monster."

We have lingered over Shakespeare's female characters who most clearly exhibit the sentiments or
illustrate the problems of chivalric love; but there
are others in whom we observe the same sweet
gravity and dignified charm that Chaucer portrays in
the Duchess Blanche. When, for example, we read
of that gentle lady's "goodly soft speech," we recall
Shakespeare's memorable lines concerning Cordelia:

> *Her voice was ever soft,*
> *Gentle and low, an excellent thing in woman.*

Chaucer says of Blanche:

> *Trouthe himself, over al and al,*
> *Had chose his maner principal*
> *In hir, that was his resting-place.*

Truth was the "dower" of Cordelia. Shakespeare also
sets the same note as Chaucer regarding love in marriage. Henry VIII praises Queen Katherine as a wife
than whom there was no better in the world, "obey-
ing in commanding;" and Brutus speaks of Portia as
Arviragus did of Dorigen: "Render me worthy of
this noble wife." Wedlock unforced, the poet states,

> *bringeth bliss,*
> *And is a pattern of celestial peace.*

Half-jestingly Biron declared:

> *Never durst poet touch a pen to write*
> *Until his ink were temper'd with love's sighs.*

Shakespeare, like Chaucer, recognized that a large
part of love-service was mere feigning—"lovers are
given to poetry; and what they swear in poetry, may
be said, as lovers, they do feign." But, like Chaucer,
he was always pleased to exalt simple, unaffected
true love, and it is that which we find embodied in
his latest creations — serene Imogen, winsome Perdita, and artless Miranda.

In only one of Shakespeare's plays is pure love

not given something of a chivalric cast; yet that is the greatest of all his poems dealing with such emotion, *Romeo and Juliet.* To be sure, we read there of the "true love's passion " of a "gentle knight " and a "true and faithful" lady; but the atmosphere that surrounds them is not mediaeval. The poet associates love and beauty in Platonic style; but he is not Italian in spirit. The love of Romeo and Juliet is of no particular age or land; it is instinctive, universal. When Shakespeare emancipates himself from the Middle Ages, he does not become a slave of the Renaissance. Wholly free, his mind fills "the world's large spaces," and in apperception he approaches the divine. Shakespeare was "myriad-minded" and could evoke any mood. Nevertheless, his constant predilection was for that love, "quick and fresh," which had "made beautiful old rhyme;" and he used "the flourish of all gentle tongues" to show it forth.

IX

SHAKESPEARE was mid-stream in the current of English literary tradition and willingly rehandled earlier chivalric themes. Among these was one of how good blood may show itself in youths obscurely reared. Guiderius and Arviragus, the sons of Cymbeline, brought up by Belarius in the forest, ignorant of their parentage, are close parallels to Sir Tor, Sir Gareth, and Sir Calidore. As early as the twelfth century,

Chrétien de Troies told the adventures of Sir Perceval with similar intent, to indicate the impulse of high lineage, and illustrate laws of chivalric life.

> *How hard it is to hide the sparks of nature!*
> *These boys know little they are sons to the King; ...*
> *They think they are mine; and, though train'd up*
> * thus meanly,*
> *I' the case wherein they bow, their thoughts do hit*
> *The roofs of palaces, and Nature prompts them,*
> *In simple and low things, to prince it much*
> *Beyond the trick of others.*

This passage, in which Belarius comments on his foster-sons, recalls that by Spenser, beginning: "O, what an easy thing is to descry the gentle blood;" but we miss the emphasis there on "mind." It is interesting to observe that when Shakespeare writes: "'T is the mind that makes the body rich," he is very near to Spenser, who makes Meliboe address Sir Calidore:

> *It is the mind that maketh good or ill,*
> *That maketh wretch or happy, rich or poor.*

Shakespeare's own key-word is "nature."

> *O thou goddess,*
> *Thou divine Nature, how thyself thou blazon'st*
> *In these two princely boys! ...*
> *   ... 'T is wonder*
> *That an invisible instinct should frame them*
> *To royalty unlearn'd, honour untaught,*
> *Civility not seen from other, valour*
> *That wildly grows in them, but yields a crop*
> *As if it had been sow'd.*

The waif Perdita, who, like Spenser's Pastorella, being reared among shepherds, "had ever learn'd to love the lowly things," also shows herself gracious and sweet, worthy of the love of courteous Florizel, whose desires ran not before his honour. The King of Bohemia, the latter's father, remarks concerning her:

> *This is the prettiest low-born lass that ever*
> *Ran on the green-sward. Nothing she does or seems*
> *But smacks of something greater than herself,*
> *Too noble for this place.*

When Perdita speaks of the art which shares with "great creating Nature," she calls forth from Polixenes the following profound words:

> *Nature is made better by no mean*
> *But Nature makes that mean ; so, over that art*
> *Which you say adds to Nature, is an art*
> *That Nature makes. You see, sweet maid, we marry*
> *A gentle scion to the wildest stock,*
> *And make conceive a bark of baser kind*
> *By bud of nobler race. This is an art*
> *Which does mend Nature, change it rather, but*
> *The art itself is Nature.*

Nature was also the "goddess" of Edmund in *King Lear*, but that traitor had only bastard virtue. Edmund remarked to unknown Edgar: "Thy tongue some say of breeding breathes;" and Albany: "Methought thy very gait did prophesy a royal nobleness." He and Kent, in disguise, like Posthumus and

Imogen, showed noble natures, tested by adversity.
Blood and virtue contended for empire in them ; their
goodness shared with their birthright. "Nature hath
meal and bran, contempt and grace."

Shakespeare believed in established degree, and
set forth his views convincingly in a long passage of
Troilus:

> *The heavens themselves, the planets, and this centre,*
> *Observe degree, priority, and place,*
> *Insisture, course, proportion, season, form,*
> *Office and custom, in all line of order.*
> *. . . O, when degree is shak'd,*
> *Which is the ladder to all high designs,*
> *The enterprise is sick! How could communities,*
> *Degrees in schools, and brotherhoods in cities,*
> *Peaceful commerce from dividable shores,*
> *The primogenitive and due of birth,*
> *Prerogative of age, crowns, sceptres, laurels,*
> *But by degree, stand in authentic place?*
> *Take but degree away, untune that string,*
> *And, hark, what discord follows! Each thing meets*
> *In mere oppugnancy.*

The poet had no drawing towards "the fool multitude that choose by show;" he had no confidence
in the judgement of the "slippery people." True, it
is blunt Casca who talks roughly of the "tag-rag
people" and the "common herd" with their "stink-
ing breath;" but the rabble in Shakespeare's plays
are always variable and prone to hasty acts, always
disposed to worship the Giant Demagogue, whom

Spenser so powerfully describes. "O thou fond many!" we read in *2 Henry IV*:

> *An habitation giddy and unsure*
> *Hath he that buildeth on the vulgar heart.*

Disgust with the mob seems to have moved him, like Chaucer, and it was, no doubt, with personal conviction that he made Henry VI speak:

> *Look, as I blow this feather from my face,*
> *And as the air blows it to me again,*
> *Obeying with my wind when I do blow,*
> *And yielding to another when it blows,*
> *Commanded always by the greater gust;*
> *Such is the lightness of you common men.*

Furthermore, Shakespeare's standards of art were consciously above those of "the million;" it was not by accident that his plays concerned themselves so largely with high-born personages, and treated notably the problems of greatness.

On the other hand, Shakespeare had strong sympathy with true aspirants to distinction, no matter from what rank they came, and believed that

> *As the sun breaks through the darkest clouds,*
> *So honour peereth in the meanest habit.*

He was aware that virtue may highly ennoble a peasant, as vice may deeply degrade a lord.

> *From lowest place when virtuous things proceed,*
> *The place is dignified by the doer's deed:*

Where great additions swell 's, and virtue none,
It is a dropsied honour. Good alone
Is good without a name. Vileness is so;
The property by what it is should go,
Not by the title. . . .
. . . That is honour's scorn
Which challenges itself as honour's born,
And is not like the sire. Honours thrive
When rather from our acts we them derive
Than our foregoers.

Here we rise to the same height that Chaucer reached, the height of true democracy. Such democracy bears no more relation to demagoguery than true to free love.

"We are gentlemen," says a knight of the court, in *Pericles:*

That neither in our hearts nor outward eyes
Envy the great nor do the low despise.

"You are right courteous knights!" is the only answer that the prince makes. According to Shakespeare, the low may be "too virtuous for the contempt of empire." In his view, blood was not opposed to virtue, fortune to merit, art to nature, nor honour to goodness; on the contrary, in each case, the one supported and confirmed the other. If we would be gentlemen, he makes clear, we must be gentle. To be gentle, however, does not necessarily mean to be intellectual. When Viola declares herself a "gentleman," Olivia remarks:

I'll be sworn thou art;
Thy tongue, thy face, thy limbs, action and spirit,
Do give thee five-fold blazon.

There is here no mention of mind.

When we reflect upon the four great writers whose works we have here studied, we find that their attitudes towards chivalry are amazingly alike, and yet characteristically different.

Chaucer's chivalry appears innate, an instinctive, ever-present check on growing worldliness, like the religious idealism implanted in a youth by a pious mother, which never ceases to control his life, even after he may have abandoned the beliefs of boyhood. It is not single-eyed, but steadily prevails in mature judgement, and is always tender and real.

Malory's chivalry reveals more emphasis on outer things. It delights in ritual; it demands adherence to a creed; it is sacerdotal, Anglican. Though it may be rigid and narrow, it stimulates earnest aspiration.

Spenser's chivalry is directed mostly towards the learned and polite. It is combined with book education, intellectual and complex. Albeit too subtle for the common run of men, it appeals persistently to the poetic, imaginative few.

Shakespeare's chivalry is retrospective; but in his works we find the ideals of the Middle Ages reproduced with full comprehension and glorified as guid-ing stars to human excellence. Shakespeare, with unique genius, widens their sphere, and makes them universal in application, meet for highest or lowest, for keenest or dullest, in this majestic world.

Chaucer presents a standard of conduct for the knight, Malory for the noble, Spenser for the courtier, and Shakespeare for the man. Their pattern figures are contrasted respectively with the coarse churl, the vulgar parvenu, the rude rustic, the common brute. Chaucer exalts worthiness, determining acts; Malory, nobility, accepting obligations; Spenser, worth, procured by self-discipline; Shakespeare, high nature, transforming character. Chaucer says "do;" Malory, "avoid;" Spenser, "study;" Shakespeare, "be."

CONCLUSION

CONCLUSION

IN the Middle Ages England borrowed chivalry from France; but English chivalry and French chivalry developed differently. In France it was chiefly restricted to a class; in England, almost from the first, it was democratized. In France, up to the Revolution, the etiquette of institutional chivalry grew increasingly important, until in the end it became largely a matter of formal politeness; in England the spirit of the ideal was so continuously insisted upon that it is now hardly separable from moral uprightness. In the one case, courtliness, refinement, elegance, careful consideration of conduct in the light of social authority, dominated its manifestation in daily life; in the other, frankness, sweetness, kindliness, subordination of self in deference to religious principle, occasioned its sway. From without inward, from inward without, these seem the contrasting methods of the two developments, both arriving, in accord with diverse national characteristics, at the same general end — distinction.

There are now those in England who insist on the benefits of class, who, if a choice were necessary, might prefer to belong to the nobility rather than to be noble, and would find greater advantage in the gentry than in gentleness; but such are few and speak in undertones. To-day even our most candid men of the world are loth to applaud Lord Chesterfield's social precepts without reserve. As a whole, Englishmen have always exalted substance more than appearance, respect more than respects, reverence more than rites. Since, as was said of them long ago, they instinctively "set their hearts' delight upon action," they have been strongly drawn to chivalry, an ideal for men of deeds. Since, however, as Burke saw, "a spirit of piety is deeply engrained in the English nation," they have persistently emphasized its moral rather than its ceremonial side.

The English ideal of the "gentleman" is an outcome of English chivalry. The word conveys to us a very different idea from the French *gentilhomme*, on which it is etymologically based. It embodies a conception more like that of the mediaeval *preud- 'omme*, indicating the aspiration, irrespective of class, which moved crusading warriors like St. Louis and Joinville. It combines the best in the attitudes of the *galant homme* and the *honnête homme*, implying courteous demeanour, but subordinating this to virtuous character. English men of rank agree that "he who is gentle should do gentle deeds;" "he is gentle who doth gentle deeds" is the creed of the majority; both groups emphasize gentle deeds as the final witness of a gentleman. If the high-born now desire to be thought worthy, they accept the best *moral* standards of the people; if the low in station desire to be

termed gentle, they accept the best *social* standards
of the aristocracy.

Emerson says that "English history is aristocracy
with the doors open." The English aristocracy, which
sets the standard of the gentleman, is composed of
elements as different as the House of Lords; it is
a class that is not confined to the bearers of titles,
any more than titles are confined to those of good
birth; it is a class in constant change. Thomas Fuller
put the matter clearly for his time (1642): "The good
yeoman is a gentleman in ore, whom the next age
may see refined; and is the wax capable of a genteel
impression, when the prince shall stamp it. Wise
Solon (who accounted Tellus the Athenian the most
happy man, for living privately on his own lands)
would surely have pronounced the English yeomanry
'a fortunate condition,' living in the temperate zone
between greatness and want, an estate of people almost peculiar to England. France and Italy are like
a die, which hath no points between cinque and ace
— nobility and peasantry. Their walls though high,
must needs be hollow, wanting filling stones. Indeed,
Germany hath her boors, like our yeomen; but, by
a tyrannical appropriation of nobility to some few
ancient families, their yeomen are excluded from ever
rising higher, to clarify their bloods. In England the
temple of honour is bolted against none who have
passed through the temple of virtue; nor is a capacity

to be genteel denied to our yeoman, who thus behaves himself."

Thackeray wrote as follows in *The Four Georges:* "Which was the most splendid spectacle ever witnessed—the opening feast of Prince George in London, or the resignation of Washington? Which is the noble character for after ages to admire—yon fribble dancing in lace and spangles, or yonder hero who sheathes his sword after a life of spotless honour, a purity unreproached, a courage indomitable, and a consummate victory? Which of these is the true gentleman? What is it to be a gentleman? Is it to have lofty aims, to lead a pure life, to keep your honour virgin; to have the esteem of your fellow citizens, and the love of your fireside; to bear good fortune meekly; to suffer evil with constancy; and through evil or good to maintain truth always? Show me the happy man whose life exhibits these qualities, and him we will salute as gentleman, whatever his rank may be; show me the prince who possesses them, and he may be sure of our love and loyalty."

Washington said of himself: "I am sensible to everything that affects the honour of a gentleman." And happily to-day in the land where he fought for independence, a land where no distinctions of class are supposed to exist, where in any case all that do exist can be transcended by individual merit or

removed by individual disgrace, the word "gentleman" still flourishes with all its English atmosphere
of superiority of Christian character. Here, as elsewhere, there attaches to good birth the presumption
of gentleness. One whose father was gentle is assumed
free of churlish offence until he shows it in his demeanour, whereas one who rises from obscurity has
to prove his title before his nobility is acknowledged.
But a sin against gentleness by one born favoured is
counted doubly foul, and a victory over disadvantage by one born without expectation meets with
peculiar acclaim. It has been agreed by final con-
sensus of opinion in this long-established democracy
that only through personal worthiness may a family
preserve, even as only so might its founder gain, the
noble name of gentle. "Lilies that fester smell far
worse than weeds!"

The whole world is kin, and something like chivalric principles can be found in every clime; but it
is wrong to state, as has recently been done by the
author of *Christian, Greek or Goth?* that chivalry
and honour are "essentially Northern," and the pro-
duct of Christianity only in so far as they are "an un-
defined and instinctive protest against it." Germanic
sentiment, particularly in respect to the attitude of
men towards women, has undoubtedly influenced
these conceptions in Germanic lands; but history
shows plainly that they developed into what they

are under the leading of Romance peoples, were fashioned first by devout Christians, and fused with the teachings of Our Lord. In Northern heathendom, warriors were sturdy, but they believed in brag; they were straightforward, but given to ferocity; to them revenge was a duty, and sweet. It was Christianity that taught Northern warriors to consecrate their strength to an impersonal ideal, to be courteous to the vanquished and avoid boast, to be meek and mild, simply because "Dieu le veut." Christian chivalry made, not for mere fulfilment of duty, but for superabundant generosity; not for simple fidelity, but for glorifying deference to women; not for rigour and harsh display of force, but for tolerance and tenderness. The finest ideal of the Christian knight, wholly unlike that of the Northern earl, was to make himself beloved. In the eighteenth century men often wrote about "Gothic chivalry," but by that they meant the institution, or ideal, which arose synchronously with the "Gothic" cathedrals; they had no thought of making it, any more than the splendid architectural monuments of mediaeval Christian aspiration, a fruit of the barbaric spirit.*

In times of national perplexity, when the *morale* of the people has seemed weak, Englishmen have often turned for new stimulus to old-time ideals of honour. It is not surprising, then, that now, when so many deplore the materialistic tendencies of the age, chivalry is being revived as a practical religion for laymen. Boy scouts are spreading some of its principles abroad in the world, and, under the inspiration of fair play, idealistic young men are beginning a new crusade against inequalities of opportunity, trying to lower the handicaps of position and power that the privileged possess. That way, perhaps, more than any other, modern chivalry tends,

> *the chivalry*
> *That dares the right, and disregards alike*
> *The yea and nay of the world.*

It is as true now as in the days of Pope:

> *Honour and shame from no condition rise;*
> *Act well your part, there all the honour lies.*

NOTES

NOTES

Page 3. Introduction to the Study of Dante, chap. viii.

Page 6. Œuvres de Froissart, i, 439.

Page 12. A different opinion is usually held. Mr. F. Warre Cornish, for example, in his valuable book on *Chivalry* (2d ed., 1908, p. 196), says of Chaucer: "Though he writes of knights and ladies, he does not properly belong to the poetry of chivalry." In the following passage (p. 231) he goes even farther: "The English language was formed in the chivalric period, and the English character, essentially the same as in the days of Alfred, expressed itself in its own speech, heightened and improved by French ideas and French words; but English literature is of a later date, and owes little to chivalry."

Page 13. "It is not at all unlikely that he was the John Chausey who, on 16th July, 1349, received a reward for bringing to Queen Philippa, at Devizes, a black palfrey from the Bishop of Salisbury, Robert Wyvill. He may have absented himself from London at this time in order to avoid the pestilence, and if so, he would no doubt take with him his wife Agnes and his young son Geoffrey, who may have been presented to the Queen on this occasion." (Kirk, *Life-Records of Chaucer,* 1900, p. xi f.) Both John and Agnes Chaucer bore arms.

Page 16. In *L'Allegro* Milton refers to Chaucer only as the author of the Squire's Tale. In his early days at least, Milton loved tales of chivalry.

Page 17. Le Joli Buisson de Jonece (Poésies, ed. Scheler, ii, 285), written about 1373.

Page 19. In Mr. B. C. Hardy's recent work, *Philippa of Hainault and Her Times* (London, 1910, p. 302), will be found Skelton's translation of the epitaph once hung near the queen's tomb in Westminster Abbey, part of which follows:

This Philippe, flowered in gifts full rare and treasures of the mind,
In beauty bright, religion, faith, to all and each most kind,
A fruitful mother Philippe was, full many a son she bred,
And brought forth many a worthy knight, hardy and full of dread;
A careful nurse to students all, at Oxford she did found
Queen's College, and Dame Pallas school, that did her fame resound.

Philippa bore Edward twelve children. Blanche, though she died so young, was the mother of seven children, of whom, however, only three lived.

Page 25. Chaucer here adopts for the nonce the tone of Jean de Meung, who says mockingly that one could not find any more Penelopes in Greece, or Lucreces in Rome. (9404 ff.) But Chaucer's general attitude towards women contrasted greatly with Jean's, the latter being of opinion that a virtuous woman was rarer than a phoenix, even than a snow-white crow, or a black swan. (9444 ff.) Chaucer puts whatever cynical remarks he repeats about women into the mouths of vulgar folk. The Merchant's Tale follows that of the Clerk!

Page 26. Chaucer translated many serious prose works: Origen's *Upon the Maudelayne;* Pope Innocent's *The Wretched Engendring of Mankind;* the Parson's Tale; and the Tale of Melibeus. His translation of Boethius appears to have been made between 1377 and 1381.

Page 28. Watriquet de Couvin said the same thing of loyalty: "C'est des vertus la plus haute, loiautez." (*Dis des Quatres Sièges,* l. 498.) Cf. also the following passage:

> De toutes vertus la greigneur
> Est loiautez en grant seigneur
> Et qui miex vaut en seignorie;
> Loiautez est d'honneur la flours;
> Humilitez, pitiez, douçours
> Sont de la loiauté mesnie;
> Loiautez est as bons amie;
> Loiautez fait chevalerie.
> (*Dis de Loiauté,* ll. 49 ff.)

Page 31. Dits de Watriquet de Couvin, ed. Scheler, 1868, pp. 43 ff., ll. 17 ff.

Page 32. Here occur the following lines:

> C'estoit la jemme et la topasse
> Des haus hommes, touz les passoit
> D'onneur faire.

One wonders if this might not have given Chaucer the suggestion to name "Thopas" the gem of a knight whom he so humorously lauds.

> Sir Thopas, he bereth the flour
> Of royal chivalry.

Page 33. See the notable exaltation of "loyalty" in Barbour's *Bruce,* ed. Skeat, E. E. T. S., II, 360 ff., etc.

Page 35. Some features of his beautiful portrait of the Parson, Chaucer found ready for his use in a French poem, the *Roman de Carité.* See Kittredge, *Mod. Lang. Notes,* XII, 113. The poet raises our admiration for the Parson by the statement:

> *But it were any persone obstinat,*
> *What-so he were, of heigh or lowe estat,*
> *Him wolde he snibben sharply for the nones.*

We read of Sir Tor in the *Morte d'Arthur* that he was "loth to do any wrong, and loth to take any wrong."

Page 37. The first thing that Joinville emphasizes when recording the "sayings and customs" of St. Louis is the latter's appeal to his son: "Win the love of thy people." Next he remarks: "The holy man so loved truth that he would not play even the Saracens false." Though, as Joinville is particular to state, Robert of Sorbonne was the "son of villain parents," yet the king would have him to dine at his table, "because of his high reputation for honour and virtue."

Page 38. "Certes, chiding may not come but out of a villain's heart." Parson's Tale, § 42. Cf. *Troilus,* Bk. v, l. 250:

> *In eche estat is litel hertes reste;*
> *God leve us for to take it for the beste.*

Page 40. Concerning backbiting, a manifestation of the foul sin of envy, the Parson says: "Some men praise their neighbours with a wicked intent; for they make alway a wicked knot at the last end. Alway they make a 'but' at the last end, that is digne of more blame, than worth is all the praising. . . . After backbiting cometh grouching, or murmuring." (§ 30.)

Page 41. This event has been cited (Skeat, III, 305) to throw light on the *Legend of Good Women* (ll. 317 ff.), where Alceste, pleading for the poet, dwells on the duties of kings. But that passage, with the allusion to the "bare shirt," seems to be derived from Watriquet's *Mireoirs as Princes.* The Parson said: "The law of Jesu Christ, that is the law of pity."

Page 43. Chaucer's attitude is evident also in the following lines, where, addressing his readers, he says, confidentially:

For if ther fille to-morwe swich a cas,
Ye knowen wel, that every lusty knight,
That loveth paramours, and hath his might,
Were it in Engelond, or elles-where,
They wolde, hir thankes, wilnen to be there.
To fighte for a lady, ben'cite!
It were a lusty sighte for to see.

Chaucer was reproved by the writer of a Scotch poem on heraldry (ca. 1494) because he represented "heralds" as recognizing Palamon and Arcite on the battlefield by their coat-armour! At the time of the war in Thebes, the Scot pointed out seriously, heralds were not yet created, nor arms "set in proper estate." See E. E. T. S., Extra Series, VIII, 1869, p. 94.

Page 44. See the *Vie du Prince Noir,* by the Chandos Herald, ll. 3794, etc.

Page 47. L'Ordene de Chevalerie, a short thirteenth-century poem, printed with translation in the Kelmscott edition of the *Order of Chivalry,* cited page 285; translated by Isabel Butler, *Tales from the Old French,* Boston, 1910, pp. 232 ff.

Page 48. Printed by Kervyn de Lettenhove, *Œuvres de Froissart,* I, 541 ff. Among the passages that remind one of Chaucer are:

Seiés ami et compaignoun
A bone gent de religioun.

Bone enfant devant la table
Doit estre cortose et serviable.

Page 49. On one occasion, for example, Sir Walter Manny and several companions placed black patches over their left eyes, and vowed not to remove them until each had distinguished himself by some worthy deed of arms. Cf. the *Vows of the Heron.*

Page 51. In the Maunciple's Tale Chaucer shows that there are some women also who have a "villain's kind," and, no matter how tenderly nurtured, will satisfy their appetites without discretion. The Maunciple begins to tell how Phebus' wife had a "lemman," when he starts at the name:

Hir lemman? certes, this is a knavish speche,
Foryeveth it me, and that I yow beseche.

Then he suddenly becomes frank, and speaks as follows:

> *I am a boistous man, right thus seye I,*
> *Ther nis no difference, trewely,*
> *Bitwixe a wyf that is of heigh degree,*
> *If of hir body dishonest she be,*
> *And a povre wenche, other than this —*
> *If it so be, they werke bothe amis —*
> *But that the gentile, in estaat above,*
> *She shal be cleped his lady, as in love;*
> *And for that other is a povre womman,*
> *She shal be cleped his wenche, or his lemman.*
> *And, God it woot, myn owene dere brother,*
> *Men leyn that oon as lowe as lyth that other.*

In the Merchant's Tale Lady May protests too much to January: "I am a gentil womman and no wenche." Chaucer is ironical in this disillusioned, "rude" tale.

Page 52. Pandarus tried to console Troilus for the loss of Cressida in the manner of the goose, assuring him that he could find plenty of ladies as fair as she. "If she be lost, we shall recover another." "The new love outchaseth oft the old." "Absence of her shall drive her out of heart." But Troilus would not listen to such leechcraft. It went in at one ear and out at the other. She who by right "inhabited" his heart should have him wholly to his death-day. He had pledged her his troth and would be hers, live or die.

Page 54. Cf. Kittredge, *Modern Philology*, IX, 467.

Page 57. Chaucer puts the 88th sonnet of Petrarch into the mouth of Troilus: "If no love is, O God, what fele I so?" (Bk. I, ll. 58-60.)

Page 60. J. A. Symonds, *Introduction to the Study of Dante,* chap. viii.

Page 63. It is doubtless true that Chaucer liked racy stories himself; but he could not have been unaware that in retelling some he also pleased John of Gaunt and other worldly folk at court. The moral Watriquet, who was also a court-poet, complained that the lords of his day paid much less attention to *example* and *bonne parole* than to *outrages* and *boufois.*

> *D'un fastras [bourde] ou d'une frivole*
> *.C. mille tans font plus grant feste*
> *Et plus tost leur entre en la teste*
> *C'uns contes de bien et d'onneur.*
>
> (*Dis de la Cygoigne,* ll. 24 ff.)

To satisfy his auditors, when they wanted him to be "of better cheer" than usual, he recited certain fabliaux, and, it must be said, with a great deal of vivacity and strong effect. It is interesting to observe that he, before Chaucer, undertook to apologize for this, lest gentle folk might think it represented his serious taste. At the end of his merry tale, the *Dis des Trois Chanoinesses de Couloigne,* he explains that there was no particular harm in the story and begs that he may not be blamed for reciting it.

> *Ainsi pris d'eles mon congié,*
> *Si mis tout cest affaire en rime*
> *Où il n'a ne honte ne rime [offence]*
> *Ne chose qui grieve à nului.*
> *Qui que le voille traire à lui*
> *(Huimais n'en puet estre autre chose),*
> *N'ai deservi qui nus m'en chose [blame];*
> *A moi ne s'en doit nus combatre:*
> *Ce sont risées pour esbatre [amuse]*
> *Les roys, les princes et les contes.*

One of the three *chanoinesses* in this tale of their debauch encouraged the poet to abandon mirth as follows:

> *Ne voulons pas choses de pris,*
> *Mais ce qui miex rire nous face.*

And Watriquet responded to their satisfaction:

> *De ce ristrent elles assez*
> *Et d'autres bons mos que je di.*

Yet we know how he felt about his work:

> *Li sens qui n'est demonstrez*
> *Par biaus diz et par fais moustrez*
> *Qu'il n'est à nullui profitans,*
> *Ne vaut riens, ne plus que li tans*
> *Qui est perdus sans recouvrer.*
> (*Dis de la Nois,* ll. 5 ff.)

There is no good reason for doubting the authenticity or sincerity of Chaucer's confession at the end of the Parson's Tale. As Sir Walter Scott says: "We must remember that we are ourselves variable and inconsistent animals."

Page 64. " I wot well," says the Parson, "there is degree above degree, as reason is: and skill (reasonable) it is that men do their devoir where it is due." (§ 66.)

Page 67. At this point in the English translation of the *Roman*, we find inserted:

> But undirstonde in thyn entent,
> That this is not myn entendement,
> To clepe no wight in no ages
> Only gentil for his linages.
> But who-so [that] is vertuous,
> And in his port nought outrageous,
> Whan sich on thou seest thee beforn,
> Though he be not gentil born,
> Thou mayst wel seyn, this is a soth,
> That he is gentil, bicause he doth
> As longeth to a gentilman;
> Of hem non other deme I can.
>
> (Ll. 2187 ff.)

If these lines are not by Chaucer, they show that others shared his opinion as to "gentlemen."

Page 68. That Chaucer in his own day was identified with such teachings is evident from the open tribute of Henry Scogan in a long ballade written soon after the "master's" death. He quotes the whole of *Gentilesse*, and enlarges upon the "virtuous sentence" that it contains. (See Skeat, *Works*, I, 82 f.) Scogan tells us that he was "father," *i.e.*, tutor, to the four sons of Henry IV.

Page 69. It may be that the poet had in mind the passage from Seneca to which the Parson refers. (§28; cf. 65, 66.)

Page 70. The translation from Guinizelli is by W. M. Rossetti, in his *Early Italian Poets;* that from Langland is by Skeat. (B Text, Passus VI, 11, 46 ff.)

Page 80. Apology for Smectymnuus (see Maccallum, *Tennyson's Idylls of the King and Arthurian Story*, p. 137). When writing, in *Paradise Lost,* of the conquering hosts of hell, Milton cannot dismiss

> what resounds
> In fable or romance of Uther's son,
> Begirt with British and Armoric knights.

And in *Paradise Regained* he alludes to

> Faery damsels met in forest wide
> By knights of Logres, or of Lyones,
> Lancelot, or Pelleas, or Pellenore.

Page 81. Professor Kittredge's article, "Who was Sir Thomas Malory?" appeared in volume v of the *Harvard Studies and Notes in*

Philology and Literature; from it the last quotation on page 82 is drawn.

Page 83. By John Rous, chantry priest and antiquary, who lived from 1411 to 1492. His work was accompanied by illustrations of peculiar interest, some of which are reproduced in Part IV of Gardiner's *A Student's History of England.* It may be worth while to call attention to the fact that Sir Gareth once lodged with a personage of the same name as the historian, the "goodly knight," the Duke de la Rowse. He was an opponent of King Arthur, and Gareth only overthrew him after "they did great battle together more than an hour and either hurt other full sore." At Gareth's wedding, "came in the Duke de la Rowse with an hundred knights with him and he did homage and fealty unto Sir Gareth, and so to hold their lands of him for ever; and he required Sir Gareth that he might serve him of the wine that day at the feast." "I will well," said Sir Gareth, "an it were better!" Almost the last words of the story are these: "And there King Arthur made the Duke de la Rowse a knight of the Round Table to his life's end and gave him great lands to spend." The source of Malory's story of Sir Gareth has not yet been discovered, but it is much more English in tone than any other part of the *Morte.* Perhaps it was a favourite in the family of Rous, and communicated by them to Malory. We remember how the story of *Pontus* was revised to suit the family of La Tour Landry.

Page 84. A picturesque duel with Sir Pandolf Malatesta, Rous tells us, brought Warwick "great laud," and he was afterwards "right worshipfully received of the Duke and lords of Venice, and many royal presents had he there given him." He also made a pilgrimage to Rome. In the Holy Land, Warwick "offered in Jerusalem at Our Lord's sepulchre, and his arms were set up on the north side of the temple, and there they remained many years after, as pilgrims that long after came there reported." Malory must have written the passage (V, 9) describing Arthur's journey to Rome, which shows large acquaintance with scenes in northern Italy on the part of the French romancer, and his final statement concerning the battles of Sir Bors and others against the Turks, with more than a translator's interest. Constantinople was captured by the Turks in 1453, and Athens in 1458.

Page 85. Fortescue was taken prisoner at the battle of Tewksbury, a few weeks after Malory's death. His *Dialogue between the*

Understanding and Faith shows him personally debating in his own mind on the misfortunes of the righteous, and other things topsy-turvy in this world.

Page 86. One is reminded of the fate of Anthony Woodville, Lord Rivers, who suffered similarly from the political struggles of the time, and during his imprisonment at Pontefract (June 25, 1483) was beheaded without trial. In prison he occupied himself with literary work, and Caxton printed his translation of *Les Dits Moraux des Philosophes* (*The Dictes and Sayings of the Philosophers*), the first book printed in England, as well as his *Cordial, or The Four Last Things,* taken from the French of Jean Mielot. Rous records some verses which, he states, Lord Rivers wrote in prison. They show the general discouragement of men of Malory's age.

Somewhat musing,	*My life was lent*
And more mourning,	*To an intent*
In remembering	*It is nigh spent.*
The unstedfastness;	*"Welcome Fortune!"*
This world being	*But I ne went*
Of such wheeling,	*Thus to be spent!*
Me contrarying,	*But she it meant!*
What may I guess?	*Such is her won(t)!*

For the whole poem, see Arber, *Dunbar Anthology,* pp. 180 ff. "Alas," said Launcelot, at the end of his life, "who may trust this world!" The noble Bors thus counsels him: "By mine advice ye shall take the woe with the weal, and take it in patience and thank God of it."

Page 92. Northumberland says, in Shakespeare's *3 Henry VI*, I, 1:

Thou art deceiv'd: 'tis not thy southern power,
Of Essex, Norfolk, Suffolk, nor of Kent,
Which makes thee thus presumptuous and proud,
Can set the duke up in spite of me.

Page 97. The *Book of the Order of Chivalry,* a fourteenth-century work, was first translated by Sir Gilbert de la Haye about 1456. In 1510 the original French text appeared in type at Lyons. See *Gilbert de la Haye's Prose MS.,* vol. i, ed. J. H. Stevenson, Scottish Text Society, 1901; ed. Abbotsford Club, 1847. Caxton's text was reprinted by F. S. Ellis, Kelmscott Press, 1892.

Page 98. Gaston Paris writes in his *Mediaeval French Literature,* p. 119: "The author of the longest prose romance in existence, the *Perceforest*, places the scenes of his narrative in England, but long before Arthur's time, and connects it with the last poems on Alexander. His work, which was composed towards 1330, at the moment the Hundred Years' War broke out, traces an ideal picture of chivalrous society, where magnificence, courtesy, bravery, the spirit of adventure and gallantry are displayed in a quantity of episodes wealthier in decorative detail than in real invention; it seems to have been long in favour with the upper classes; frequently copied in the fifteenth century, in spite of its enormous extent, it was printed in the sixteenth, and has considerably contributed the images that in modern times are fashioned of ancient chivalry."

Page 103. The prologue to the Book of Hawking in the *Book of St. Albans,* by Dame Juliana Berners (printed at St. Albans in 1486; facsimile by William Blades, London, 1881), reads in part as follows: "In so much that gentlemen and honest persons have great delight in hawking and desire to have the manner to take hawks. . . . Therefore this book following in a due form shows very knowledge of such pleasure to gentlemen and persons disposed to see it." The prologue to Mistress Barnes' compilation on hunting begins thus: "Likewise, as in the Book of Hawking aforesaid are written and noted the terms of pleasure belonging to gentlemen having delight therein, in the same manner this book following showeth to such gentle persons the manner of hunting for all manner of beasts, whether they be beasts of venery, or of chase, or rascal."

Even now the subject of the danger to hunting because of the new, so-called "socialistic" legislation in England is occupying the public press. The following hectic paragraph appeared in the *Continental Daily Mail,* January 12, 1911, under the heading, "A Gloomy Forecast:" "The twenty odd millions circulated so freely and to such good purpose annually through Great Britain on hunting alone, will circulate no more; starvation, the workhouse and bankruptcy will stare thousands of honest people in the face, as the healthy, manly sport of our fathers dies an ignominious death. No greater misfortune could befall the nation, both from a financial and physical point of view, than to put an end to or even a check on sport, and hunting in particular. Manliness, pluck, endurance, generosity, all characteristics of the English race, have been inherited mainly through our forefathers' love for hardy out-door sport."

Page 107. Probably Malory felt as Sir David Lyndesay wrote in *Squire Meldrum:*

> *I think it is no happy life*
> *A man to jape his master's wife,*
> *As did Launcelot; this I conclude*
> *Of such amour could come no good.*

Elaine thus rebuked the queen: "Alas, madam, ye do great sin, and to yourself great dishonour, for ye have a lord of your own, and therefore it is your part to love him."

Page 111. An excellent rendering of this work has just appeared in a volume of translations of fourteenth-century alliterative poems by Miss Jessie L. Weston, entitled *Romance, Vision, and Satire.* (Houghton Mifflin Co., Boston, 1912.)

Page 117. Peacham, in 1634, thus emphasizes the importance of heraldry: "It is meet that a noble, or gentleman who beareth arms, and is well descended, be not only able to blazon his own proper coat, derive by pedigree the descent of his family from the original, know such matches as are joined to him in blood; but also of his prince, the nobility and gentry where he liveth; which is not of mere ornament, as the most suppose, but diversely necessary and of great consequence: as had I fortuned to have lived in those times when that fatal difference of either Rose was to be decided by the sword, with which party in equity and conscience could I have sided, had I been ignorant of the descent and pedigree royal, and where the right had been by inheritance of blood, match, or alliance?" (*Compleat Gentleman,* ed. G. S. Gordon, 1906, chap. xv, p. 160.)

Page 121. Malory includes Solomon and Joshua among "knights of chivalry." (Bk. XVII, 5, 6.)

Page 144. Sir William Temple says in his essay *Of Poetry:* "Spenser endeavoured . . . to make instruction instead of story the subject of an epic poem. His execution was excellent, and his flights of fancy very noble and high, but his design was poor, and his moral lay so bare that it lost the effect: 'tis true, the pill was gilded, but so thin that the colour and the taste were too easily discovered."

Page 151. Milton says, in *Comus:*

> *Virtue could see to do what virtue would*
> *By her own radiant light.*

Page 152. Tennyson says, in *Oenone:*

> *Self-reverence, self-knowledge, self-control,*
> *These three alone lead life to sovereign power.*

Page 153. Hoby's version was printed, with an Introduction by Walter Raleigh, in the *Tudor Translations,* London, 1900. In Hoby's opinion, the *Courtier* was: "To men grown in years, a pathway to the beholding and nursing of the mind, and to whatsoever else is meet for that age; to young gentlemen, an encouraging to garnish their mind with moral virtues, and their body with comely exercises, and both the one and the other with honest qualities to attain unto their noble end: to ladies and gentlewomen, a mirror to deck and trim themselves with virtuous conditions, comely behaviours and honest entertainment toward all men: and to them all in general, a storehouse of most necessary implements for the conversation, use, and training-up of man's life with courtly demeanours."

Page 156. There is much, perhaps, that is merely literary in Spenser's diatribes against court life. But Languet wrote to Sidney after a visit to England: "It appeared to me that the manners of your court are less manly than I could wish; and the majority of your great folk struck me as more eager to gain applause by affected courtesy, than by such virtues as benefit the commonwealth, and are the chief ornament of *noble minds and high-born personages.*" He warned Sidney lest he "come by habit to care for things which soften and emasculate our mind." See Symonds' *Life of Sidney,* p. 62.

As has been well said: "It was not from a passion for learning for its own sake, nor from a wish to dignify outward life and leisure; not from a national instinct for a great past; not from a desire to reform doctrine or ceremony in religion; but first and foremost to meet a demand for better governance, to call into play, from new sources as well as from old, forces better equipped for the more complex tasks of the modern State; it was for such an end, practical, and in a certain sense, limited, that the Englishmen first grasped the weapons which the Renaissance held out to them from Italy." (W. H. Woodward, *Education during the Renaissance,* 1906, p. 301.)

Page 157. Brunetto Latini wrote concerning *gentilezza :*

> *In sooth there are persons of high condition*
> *Who call themselves "noble:" all others they hold cheap*

Because of this nobility. . . .

　　. . . *He who endures not toil*
For honour's sake, let him not imagine that he comes
Among men of worth, because he is of lofty race;
For I hold him noble who shows that he follows the path
Of great valour and of gentle nurture,—
So that, besides his lineage, he does deeds of worth,
And lives honourably so as to make himself beloved.

　　　(Translated by W. M. Rossetti, *Italian Courtesy Books*, E. E. T. S.,
　　　E. S., VIII, 1869, Pt. II, p. 12, from the *Tesoretto*, written in Paris be-
　　　tween 1260 and 1265.)

Page 161. It is not, of course, meant that Spenser derived his
ideas directly from the Greek. They came to him in the main
from Italian sources. See J. B. Fletcher, *The Religion of Beauty in
Woman, and Other Essays on Platonic Love in Poetry and Society.*
New York, 1911, 116 ff.; J. S. Harrison, *Platonism in English
Poetry*, New York, 1903; and Professor Courthope's admirable
chapter on Spenser in the *Cambridge History of English Literature*, III, 211 ff.

Page 174. One of the most renowned French works on conduct
was Alain Chartier's *Bréviaire des Nobles.*

Page 175. Peacham wrote: "Nobility then (taken in the general
sense) is nothing else than a certain eminency, or notice taken
of some one above the rest, for some notable act performed, be
it good or ill; and in that sense are *nobilis* and *ignobilis* usually
among the Latin poets taken. More particularly, and in the genuine sense, nobility is the honour of blood in a race or lineage,
conferred formerly upon some one or more of that family, either
by the prince, the laws, or customs of that land or place, whereby
*either out of knowledge, culture of the mind, or by some glorious
action performed,* they have been useful and beneficial to the
commonwealths and places where they live. For since *all virtue
consisteth in action,* and no man is born for himself, we add, beneficial and useful to his country; for hardly they are to be admitted for noble, who (though of never so excellent parts) con-
sume their light, as in a dark lantern, in contemplation, and a
stoical retiredness. And since *honour is the reward of virtue and
glorious actions* only, vice and baseness must not expect her favours. . . . Nobility hangeth not upon the airy esteem of vulgar
opinion, but is indeed of itself essential and absolute. Beside,
nobility being inherent and natural, can have (as the diamond)
the lustre but only from itself; honours and titles externally con-

ferred are but attendant upon desert and are but as apparel, and the drapery to a beautiful body. . . . *Learning is an essential part of nobility.* . . . Who is nobly born and a scholar withal deserveth double honour." Peacham found Sir Kenelm Digby "noble and absolutely complete." Though a cavalier, he omits all mention of courtly love. Milton was not the only one in his age whose attitude towards women was not one of mediaeval respect.

Page 196. Another example of fair play occurs in *2 Henry VI*, IV, 10, 45 ff., where Iden speaks to Jack Cade:

> *Nay, it shall ne'er be said, while England stands,*
> *That Alexander Iden, an esquire of Kent,*
> *Took odds to combat a poor famish'd man.*

Page 215. The Buke of the Law of Armys was edited by J. H. Stevenson for the Scottish Text Society in 1901. (*Gilbert of the Haye's Prose MS.*, vol. i.) Bonet's last bit of counsel is: "A king should be temperate and measured in his conversation, and not repair among folk in places public over ofttimes. For anything that [the] commons see over oft, they prize all the less. And when it is *seldom seen*, it gives folk in more great desire to see it again, aye more and more. And for this cause the great Sultan of Babylon comes but thrice in the year in public audience forward. And then, when he comes forward on three *festival* days, he comes riding with such a *state and solemnity* that all the people desire and press the more to see him [than if] he rode every day, or every week, or month." Shakespeare makes Henry IV dwell at particular length on this same subject:

> *Had I so lavish of my presence been,*
> *So common-hackney'd in the eyes of men,*
> *So stale and cheap to vulgar company,*
> *Opinion, that did help me to the crown,*
> *Had still kept loyal to possession*
> *And left me in reputeless banishment,*
> *A fellow of no mark nor likelihood.*
> *By being seldom seen, I could not stir*
> *But like a comet I was wonder'd at;*
>
> . . . .
>
> *Thus did I keep my person fresh and new,*
> *My presence, like a robe pontifical,*
> *Ne'er seen but wonder'd at; and so my* state,
> *Seldom but sumptuous, showed like a* feast,
> *And won by rareness such* solemnity.

(*1 Henry IV*, III, 2, 39 ff.)

Bonet wrote: "A king should not over lightly trow all tales nor sudden tidings. For many liars ofttimes flatter lords with false tales, and set them in wrong and evil purpose." Prince Hal pleads:

> Such extenuation let me beg
> As, in reproof of many tales devis'd,
> Which oft the ear of greatness needs must hear,
> By smiling pick-thanks and base newsmongers.
>
> (III, 2, 22 ff.)

Bonet dwells upon the necessity of a king's showing justice without favour to anyone whatsoever, citing the example of a prince who would not alter the judgement properly passed upon his own son, by which he should forfeit his two eyes. We recall how Henry V, addressing the Chief Justice, quotes his father's remark:

> "Happy am I, that have a man so bold
> That dares do justice on my proper son."
>
> (2 Henry IV, V, 2, 108 f.)

Bonet emphasizes that "first and foremost [a king] should come to his realm through righteous title of right succession; for, and he do not, the end may not be good nor the governance honourable." Henry IV, in anguish on his death-bed, tells of the misfortunes that had followed his usurpation of power:

> God knows, my son,
> By what by-paths and indirect crook'd ways
> I met this crown; and I myself know well
> How troublesome it sat upon my head.
>
> (IV, 5, 184 ff.)

Bonet tells the story of the king who was unwilling to be crowned. "And when the diadem was presented to him, he took it in his hand, and said that all men might hear, with tears falling from his eyes, O diadem!... And men wist what great charge and little profit, what mickle peril and wretchedness follows thee, suppose thou wert lying on the earth, he would not uptake thee with thy charges and perils." Henry IV felt strongly that "Uneasy lies the head that wears a crown," and Prince Hal, when he observes the crown beside his dying father, exclaims:

> Why doth the crown lie there upon his pillow,
> Being so troublesome a bedfellow?
> O polish'd perturbation! golden care!
> That keep'st the ports of slumber open wide
> To many a watchful night!
>
> (IV, 5, 21 ff.)

Bonet says: "I should not over highly exhort kings and princes to do justice, but rather to mercy and grace. For that is a king's proper condition, to aye justice with mercy mell [mingle], after as he sees cause pitiable, and as the case requires; for that is clemency, that is the fairest point of a king's crown."

Portia thus addresses Shylock:

> [*Mercy*] *becomes*
> *The throned monarch better than his crown.*
> *His sceptre shows the force of temporal power,*
> *The attribute to awe and majesty,*
> *Wherein doth sit the dread and fear of kings;*
> *But mercy is above the sceptred sway,*
> *It is enthroned in the hearts of kings,*
> *It is an attribute to God himself;*
> *And earthly power doth then show likest God's*
> *When mercy seasons justice.*
>
> (IV, 1, 188 ff.)

Cf. *Measure for Measure*, II, 2, 59 ff.

Whether or no the parallels pointed out here and in the text convince the reader that Shakespeare knew the *Law of Arms*, they unquestionably show (which is after all the important point) that he gave particular thought to questions which were discussed by writers on chivalry as early as the fourteenth century.

Page 224. George Gascoigne, in his *Delicate Diet for Dainty-mouthed Drunkards* (1576), says: "Drunkenness is a great evil and an odious sin unto God; yet it is so grown in use, with many men through the whole world, that, with such as will not understand God's commandments, it is now taken to be no great sin. . . . I would (for God) that our gentry, and the better sort of our people, were not so much acquainted with quaffing, carousing, and drinking of hearty draughts, at many merry conventions. Would God that we learned not (by the foreleaders before-named) to charge and conjure each other unto the pledge, by the name of such as we most honour and have in estimation. Alas! we Englishmen can mock and scoff at all countries for their defects, but before they have many times mustered before us, we can learn by little and little to exceed and pass them all, in all that which (at first sight) we accounted both vile and villainous. . . . We were wont (in times past) to contemn and condemn the *Almaines* and other of the low countries, for their beastly drinking and quaffing. But nowadays, although we use it not daily like them (for it seems that they are naturally inclined unto that vice), yet, when we do make banquets and merriments, as we term them, we surpass them very far; and small difference is found betwixt us and them, but only that they (by a custom rooted amongst them, and become next cousin to nature as beforesaid) do daily wallow in a gross manner of beastliness, and we think to cloak the filthiness thereof by a more honourable solemnity, and by the cleanly title of courtesy. (*Works*, ed. Cunliffe, Cambridge, 1910, II, 457.)

Peacham wrote later: "Within these fifty or threescore years it was a rare thing with us in England to see a drunken man, our nation carrying the name of the most sober and temperate of any other in the world. But since we had to do in the quarrel of the Netherlands, about the time of Sir John Norrice, his first being there, the custom of drinking and pledging healths was brought over into England: Wherein let the Dutch be their own judges if we equal them not; yes, I think rather excel them." (*Compleat Gentleman*, ed. Gordon, p. 229.)

In *Othello* (II, 3, 80 ff.) Shakespeare makes Iago state that in England "they are most potent in potting; your Dane, your German, and your swag-belli'd Hollander . . . are nothing to your English. . . . Why, he drinks you, with facility, your Dane dead drunk; he sweats not to overthrow your Almain; he gives your Hollander a vomit ere the next pottle can be filled." Cf. *Hamlet*, I, 2, 175. In the *Book of St. Albans* we read that one of the "nine vices contrary to gentlemen" is "to be full of drinking and drunkenly."

Page 230. We are reminded of Langland (see above, page 70) when we read Hamlet's remarks in the graveyard: "By the Lord, Horatio, these three years I have taken note of it; the age has grown so picked that the toe of the peasant comes so near the heel of the courtier, he galls his kibe."

Page 272. Sir Walter Scott says, in his *Essay on Chivalry:* "The habits derived from the days of chivalry still retain a striking effect on our manners, and have fully established a graceful as well as useful punctilio, which tends on the whole to the improvement of society. Every man enters the world under the impression, that neither his strength, his wealth, his station, nor his wit will excuse him from answering, at the risk of his life, any unbecoming encroachment on the civility due to the weakest, the poorest, the least important, or the most modest member of the society in which he mingles. All, too, in the rank and station of gentlemen are forcibly called upon to remember, that they must resent the imputation of a voluntary falsehood as the most gross injury; and that the rights of the weaker sex demand protection from every one who would hold a good character in society. In short, from the wild and overstrained courtesies of chivalry has been derived our present system of manners."

72517

DATE DUE

GAYLORD

PRINTED IN U.S.A.